Reiki
Hold My Beer,
I've Got This!

Phillip Hawkins

Reiki Master Teacher Trainer Assessor
Student of Reiki and Life

Copyright

Front cover design by: Barry Hamilton

Work by the Same Author

Reiki: One student to another

The Kid who couldn't fit in

Better to be freed by the truth than held captive by a lie

Pink is the new Black: When an old hurt becomes a new healing

Psychic Development: Reflections on a theme #4

Psychic Development: Reflections on a theme #3

Wisdom of the Ancients: Reflections on a theme #2

Reiki: Reflections on a theme #1

Table of Contents

Introduction

If you have chosen to read this book in the hope of learning about Reiki you won't be disappointed, but if you expect to hear the same old clichéd story that has been done to death, you most certainly will be. This book is 100% Reiki, stripped back and unplugged from mainstream preconceived and conditioned ideas of what it is, and how it's supposed to be taught and used.

Don't get me wrong tradition has its rightful place for the past, present and future are siblings, the same family, just different generations that have a different sets of values. Tradition can provide a rock solid foundation, but when set in stone it becomes rigid and inflexible unable to change, and resentful of those who choose to do so. Tradition has its place in our cultural, social and personal development, but it must never be at the expense of knowledge and understanding. If not, it's just another piece of unnecessary baggage we struggle to carry.

As a Reiki ''Master'' teacher with the best part of twenty years experience working with Reiki and trained in the traditional Usui way, I have to say some of the myths and misconceptions are nothing more than bullshit and ''old wives tales'' lacking substance and fail miserably to stand up to scrutiny. In the beginning, I accepted it all hook, line and sinker; I never questioned any of it primarily because I was told that as a student it was not up to me to question the facts, but to simply accept the word of my Reiki Masters as gospel. Years down the line as an experienced teacher trainer I recognise this approach as indoctrination rather than education, which is the true nature and expression of Reiki.

Although I have all of the accreditation necessary to claim the title of Master I prefer not to do so. I am a teacher first and foremost, and I have to be honest I find the title Master more than a little pretentious, but I fully support any Reiki Master, including my own students who wish to claim that title as their own. What may come as a shock to some but not to those who know me, I don't consider myself a healer in the traditional sense of the word. The Reiki I teach my students is the only person we can ''heal'' is ourselves, which is only possible through the acquisition and application of knowledge and understanding of who we are, and the quality of life we create through the choices we make.

**The only person
we can "heal" is ourselves**

If someone comes to me and says ''I want to be a healer'' I ask them to first heal themselves and then come back to me when they have done so. Obviously, this isn't what they expected to hear and causes more than a little confusion, but it creates the space and opportunity to explain the true nature of illness and disease and what is required to bring about healing in mind, body and spirit. If my approach resonates with them they stay and learn, if not they usually seek out a teacher that is compatible with their needs and I am totally ok with that. What is important is that the student finds a teacher and learns something, even if it's not what I myself believe in. Our freewill is sacrosanct for without it any form of conscious personal development is impossible. We help those we can, and bless the ones we are unable to.

Chapter 1 - Reiki's place in the 21st century

Reiki works if not in the way we think it does. Experience has taught me that the energy we have labelled Reiki is neither invasive nor dictatorial and at the risk of alienating myself from some of my fellow Reiki teachers and practitioners, I have to say that Reiki is not the miracle cure many think it is, and was never meant to be promoted as such.

Reiki is not the miracle cure many think it is, and was never meant to be promoted as such.

Although universal, it's still no more than an expression of the source that created it and as such it has neither the desire nor the authority to override our free will or negate our freedom of choice. Freewill and the freedom to choose is the cornerstone of all personal, social and spiritual development and are fundamental in the healing process. Reiki is accredited with being and doing many wonderful things, but what it's not is invasive or dictatorial and to those who say 'it changed my life' I'm sorry but I have to say it didn't at least not in the way you think it did. If your life has changed it's because you took the steps necessary to change and it changed as a consequence of your actions. Reiki may have played a part by helping to raise your awareness and accept that options were available to you, but ultimately it's your life and it's your responsibility to live it. Put simply if we want something different then we must do something different. As Gandhi said 'we must become the change we desire'.

Reiki may be viewed as a spiritual and altruistic discipline but it must conform to the universal and spiritual laws that give it form and purpose, for the created can never be greater than its creator. Reiki is just one expression of a divine consciousness and if as we say, it's universal then it has to be current, contemporary, and relevant to modern day needs of the individual and society as a whole. Tradition is a wonderful thing and has its place but it should never be used as an excuse for the perpetuation of outdated ideas and ideals, and our Reiki practice has to keep pace with present day knowledge and understanding of health, and the healing of illness and disease.

Medical science has moved on since the days of Dr Usui and whether we like it or not we have to deal with the challenges of living in the twenty first century. Spirituality like tradition has its place in modern day life, and if science provides the medical knowledge then spirituality has to provide a deeper understanding of the role we play in securing our own health and well-being. This underpins the Reiki precept that the only person we can heal is ourselves. We need to educate ourselves to understand what healing is, and how Reiki can assist in bringing about this change in our physical, mental and emotional condition that we call healing.

In an attempt to heal ourselves ~~change~~ requires choices to be made which is a process of transition. The common denominator for this change of heart and mind can be Reiki and the education it brings. This is why knowledge and understanding are a pre-requisite for the necessary changes to take place so that healing of self can come about. Knowledge of oneself and the knowledge and expertise of health care professionals who can help facilitate the healing process to take place.

There was a time in our not so long and distant past when we were encouraged to believe that God caused us to be ill if we had sinned, the illness was a punishment for the perceived sin and motivation to change our evil ways. The more ''enlightened'' of the time believed that science and not religion held the answer to the causes of illness and disease. The answer was they said in the stars; if the alignment of the sun and planets were changed we suffered illness and disease because of that celestial disruption.

During this period of global intellectual and educational darkness the vast majority of people depended for medical knowledge and care on local amateurs with no professional training, but with a reputation as wise healers who could diagnose problems and give sick people advice what to do. Thankfully in the current age of enlightenment not a week goes by without news of a new medical breakthrough, yet people's general health is now in

17

decline with the average person's life expectancy in deep recession and heading towards a modern day dark age of illness and disease of epidemic proportions. It would appear that scientific knowledge is no guarantee of a long and healthy life, nor is a life of abundance, of wealth and prosperity or technological advancement.

The twenty first century gifts us so much yet appears to be exacting such a heavy price on our health and well-being. The twenty first century is in dire need of a magic formula that will help eradicate heart disease, strokes, cancer, obesity, dementia, alcohol, and smoking related deaths of epidemic proportions. Nearly all of which are now accepted as the result of lifestyle choices we are making on a daily basis. This miracle comes not as a pill but in the form of education in the community and society as a whole. Educating people to be aware of the consequences of their actions, and take personal responsibility for their health and well-being. Empowering them to make life and health affirming choices; this is healing through knowledge and understanding, it's truth demonstrated. Reiki is not a miracle cure all; it will not do it for you, it will not live your life for you or make the changes that only you can make in order to experience healing. It's not in the business of making stuff disappear as if by magic, if anything it will do just the opposite.

> Reiki is not a miracle cure all; it will not do it for you, it will not live your life for you or make the changes that only you can make in order to experience healing.

It will take what is hidden or which you refuse to acknowledge and shine the light of knowledge and understanding on it. In doing so its saying "ok this is what we need to deal with in order for healing to come about, I will help if you need me but it's your stuff and you will have to deal with it". Healing is a process not a magic formula; it's a transition from point A to point B with a multiple of increments on the improvement scale and the more knowledge and understanding we acquire and implement the more progress can be made. Doing the things that affirm health and well-being and letting go of stuff that has a harmful effect, stopping the things that may be socially acceptable but literally puts our health and life at risk. When we first come to Reiki we can buy into the spiritual side of it for all of the right reasons and usually that's because it fulfils a need within us and human nature being what it is we all like to be associated with success and feel part of something that's important and much bigger than ourselves. What could be bigger than playing a part in healing the world?

However if we study the Reiki small print we will see that it says quite clearly the only person we can heal is ourselves, so the best we can hope for is that the world learns to heal one person at a time. This process of learning is defined as 'education' and is healing by another name.

As science evolves so spirituality must also keep pace and provide a counter balance to the scientific ''how it is'' with a much needed spiritual ''why it is'' which is usually for the good of mankind. Spirituality, and Reiki as an expression of that knowledge and understanding has a place in the 21st century and a job to do, but we can only work effectively as Reiki teachers and practitioners if we have a clear understanding of what Reiki is and the role we have to play. We are educators first and foremost and it's in that role that we help facilitate the healing process through the assimilation of knowledge and understanding. Dr Usui learned through his own personal experience that sustained healing requires the patient to let go of the victim mentality, play an active part in their life, and take the lead in their own healing so that it becomes meaningful, personal, and sustained.

> Sustained healing requires the patient to let go of the victim mentality, play an active part in their life and take the lead in their own healing.

I know from personal experience that Reiki works but I'm under no illusions as to its relationship with the laws of cause and effect that incorporates freedom of choice and our free will. On a personal level the meaning of all life is whatever we want it to be, reflecting as we grow spiritually a higher consciousness and level of awareness through a process of continual development and the recognition of our true spiritual identity. Living is a learning process, if not it's a life wasted. Lessons are learnt through experiences chosen by default through ignorance and fear, or through knowledge and understanding and the opportunity to learn from our mistakes and move forward. Reiki isn't some kind of esoteric cleaning product that has a new and improved formula designed to take all of the hard work out of cleaning house and home. It's not designed to miraculously wipe away the accumulated debris caused by years of misuse, abuse and neglect in one effortless sweep.

Yes, it has the power to get into all those nooks and crannies, those out of the way places that rarely if ever see the light of day where all of the dirt and debris collects, or placed out of sight and out of mind. To help clean the house and home that is you, it must first get your attention and make you aware of the work that needs to be carried out by you in order that you can appreciate value and understand the cleansing healing process that's taking place.

Chapter 2 - Are we freed by the truth, or attached to a lie

When we challenge what we hold to be true we sometimes come up with a few surprises that can shatter our belief system completely leaving us demoralised and disillusioned, or it can free us from conditioning and set us on a new path of learning. Research into the history and development of Reiki throws up some interesting facts that go un-noticed, or are ignored because they don't sit well with the Reiki story we choose to teach or believe in.

Usui attuned or empowered himself through personal study and the realisation he was, and always had been connected to the power of the universe, that would later be labelled ''Reiki''. He didn't call it Reiki, his successors did, he referred to it as ''his system'', he didn't use symbols as such, and when he did it was nothing more than a teaching aid to give students a point of focus and to help them visualise a concept such as energy follows intent. It was never promoted as a healing discipline of others; it was, is and always will be primarily a means of personal spiritual development. When we begin to improve the quality of our thoughts, beliefs and the choices we act upon, our health and well-being begins to improve in relation to our commitment to our personal development. Once we have learnt to help ourselves we are then in a position to help others help/heal themselves through the sharing of knowledge and understanding.

Reiki was, is and always will be primarily a means of personal spiritual development.

One of the greatest myths perpetuated about Reiki is that it is a miracle cure all with magical powers to heal everything it touches. This is partly due to misunderstanding and a misconception of the nature of Reiki, and partly due to the fact that promoting it as such makes it a very desirable commodity and generates a great deal of income for those who have an invested interest in this misplaced belief system. This concept is far more appealing that the reality we are faced with on a daily basis. Yes it helps relieve the effects of stress, anxiety and tension but if we use this as "'proof'" of healing we are overlooking some very important and key issues. Stress, anxiety and tension  are nothing more than symptoms, superficial in relation to the often deep seated underlying cause that goes untouched and unrecognised. Once the euphoria of training or treatment begins to wane and the placebo effect wares off, the cause remains untouched and deep rooted as ever.

Then we are faced with a crisis all of our own making. Is it that Reiki doesn't work and we have bought into a lie, has the Reiki Master left out some key information, or is the student to blame for not using Reiki properly, or all of the above. The reality is it's all of them and at the same time, none of them. Does Reiki work, undoubtedly? Do I have faith in the fact that it works, no because faith is a substitute for knowledge and understanding and I know from personal experience and that of my students and clients that it works, albeit not in the way most believe it to. Reiki is neither dictatorial nor intrusive; it has neither the authority nor the desire to over ride our free will and force itself upon us, to remove the symptom whilst leaving a cause created by ignorance and fear untouched.

Reiki doesn't remove it uncovers, it clears away the confusion to help us recognise and identify the underlying causes that need our attention in order that we can begin to help and heal ourselves. The belief that Reiki is a miracle cure is far more palatable to most people, and easier than the reality of helping you to get your shit together. It will help you identify it, and deal with it, but it's team work and it won't do it all for you. It's about empowerment but not in the way you have been led to believe. As a Reiki teacher, my role is to make you aware that you are already connected to the power of the universe, you always have been. I can't connect what is already connected to the source; my role is to make you aware of that fact and help you accept the responsibility and duty of care you have for your own life. This is true empowerment; it can't be given, only accepted by the individual once they awaken to their true spiritual identity and the creative power within themselves.

The belief that Reiki is a miracle cure is far more palatable to most people, and easier than the reality of helping you to get your shit together.

The Reiki I teach is one of personal responsibility of self and their learning, of personal power and personal development, and as such those who commit to this training programme are guaranteed a level of success in direct relation to the time and effort they commit to their personal development.

Chapter 3 - Dr Education, the new healer in town

Regardless of the level of training achieved all Reiki practitioners are educators first and foremost. Regardless of the healing discipline, knowledge and understanding is a pre-requisite for without it healing of any description is impossible. Knowledge and understanding are powerful physicians; they educate and empower us to make the necessary changes in order to improve our quality of life, health and well-being. Without knowledge and understanding, ignorance and fear will prevail and provide the darkness necessary for a multitude of illnesses and disease to become established and grow.

It is said if you give a man a fish you feed him for a day, teach him to fish and you feed him for a lifetime. If we teach mankind to think for itself it will discover within the power to feed, nourish and ultimately change the world.

Unfortunately, knowledge and understanding never comes to us complete; and it has to be said neither does personal development. A journey like any other; a journey of progress and delays, a journey of detours and dead ends, moments of elation when I could see so clearly; and dark days when I felt lost and overwhelmed by despair. Companions have been many, and each one has contributed to my personal development, their words of wisdom and encouragement have helped guide my faltering steps ever forward. Some challenged the beliefs I held about myself and dared me to come to the edge and fly. Writing has provided a freedom of expression and enabled me to become the author and narrator to my own life story, when pain and suffering silenced the damaged inner child who even now so many years later still seeks to be heard.

 This chapter in my life story is a part of this evolutionary process, a milestone that helps me gain perspective and direction. It also helps me to look back free from the emotional baggage carried for so long, to see just how far I have come. In sharing this experience I hope you the reader will journey with me for a while and in doing so help one another find our path on this journey we call life. Indoctrination forcibly instils ideas, attitudes and beliefs by coercion, the indoctrinated person doesn't question or critically examine the belief system they have been forced to learn. Education by comparison is personal development by means of academic and experiential study and practice, usually under supervision of a teacher or mentor. Education is not about telling the student what to think, but empowering them to think objectively for themselves, and where necessary challenging what they hold to be true.

> Education is not about telling the student what to think, but empowering them to think objectively for themselves, and where necessary challenging what they hold to be true.

Education asks us to loosen our grip on reality and embrace the unknown, but sometimes before we can educate ourselves we have to unpick the ties and lies indoctrination uses to manipulate and control us.

Sometime during your search for personal development, you may be presented with a new idea, belief or value that you just can't accept, causing you an uncomfortable amount of mental and emotional distress. In psychology this condition is called *cognitive dissonance* and occurs when a person is faced with two or more contradictory beliefs, ideas or values. This is why if we don't really believe at a deep and meaningful level the changes we are being asked to accept, we will automatically revert back to the old ways at the first opportunity. We are creatures of habit and routine and we find comfort in internal consistency. Conflicting ideals creates inconsistency and makes us feel uncomfortable and we will do anything to reduce that dissonance, or actively avoid the cause of the discomfort. We will reject the idea or the action that could cause us to change what we hold to be true.

Knowing this, the duty of any teacher is to educate. We do this, not by telling the student what to think, but by challenging what they already hold to be true. Our role is to guide and help them break free of ignorance and fear formed by conditioning, tradition, and dogma. We dare them to consider new thoughts and ideas that have the power to change their perception of reality and in doing so they can begin to take responsibility for their own learning. It is said that 'we teach what we wish to learn' and in many ways this is true, for knowledge and understanding never comes to us complete, and on our journey of exploration to find the truth, knowledge and understanding helps illuminate the path that opens up before us as the teacher and student walk side by side. A teacher never seeks to condition or control; they seek to empower by helping the student to free their spirit, and their mind. Their questions should never be seen as a challenge to authority but as an expression of their desire to learn and understand.

A teacher never seeks to condition or control; they seek to empower by helping the student to **free their spirit, and their mind**.

The dark ages of mankind were unable to hold captive those who had the courage to question what was then held to be true, and overcome the barriers to development, real or imaginary. Education is a physician of the mind and the body, for without the attendance of knowledge and understanding healing of the person is impossible and their fate is left in the hands of ignorance and fear. Symptoms of ignorance and fear may be addressed on a superficial level, but the root cause will go untouched. A closed mind is unaware of its own ignorance and the self-imposed limitations that restrict its development and growth. Changed against its will, it remains connected to its roots and will at the first opportunity seek to return to the comfort of the beliefs and values it holds to be true. Education is the only viable means of introducing and maintaining sustainable change in the individual and in society as a whole. Reward and punishment are limited in their concept and application, as with any addiction their use and application will have to be increased in order to maintain a level of control. Empower a person to take responsibility to think for themselves and you help free them from the control of conditioning, tradition, and dogma and the many prejudices they help perpetuate. Every student has a personal best and it's the role of the teacher to help them achieve it whatever it may be.

Everyone has the capacity to learn but some may not be ready and willing to do so, as teachers we help those that we can and gently sow the seeds of learning that one day  may come to fruition in another time, another place and with teacher who is better suited to the needs of the developing student. Like ripples spreading out beyond our horizon to rest upon far distant shores, knowledge and understanding has the power to transcend time and affect in a positive and life affirming way the lives of generations to come.

Chapter 4 - All this spiritual shit will change me, won't it?

Words and inspirational mantras will change my life, won't they? Sorry they won't. We often hear that certain words or meaningful phrases are powerful enough to change your life once you have read them. Unfortunately, words in themselves don't have the power to change your life. Life changes; circumstances may change, but ultimately people change as a consequence of actions taken. Words are signposts that can help redirect our thoughts, hopefully resonating with us in such a way that they stimulate a re-evaluation of what we hold to be true and the way we live our lives. Change can be evolutionary or revolutionary, but change of any description requires a catalyst that's instrumental in triggering the change process. Inspirational words can act as that catalyst but they require two other components to bring about change. If words act as signposts, then hopefully they will help us to find within ourselves the desire for change and a willingness to take action. The value of signposts lies in their ability to give direction, but no matter how informative they can never make the journey for us, and we alone can take the steps necessary to change the direction our life takes.

When it comes to learning, we are all different. We not only learn in different ways, we have different speeds in the way we can process and retain new information. Whether we realise it or not we all have blind spots when it comes to changing our beliefs and the way we think, which is exactly how we are supposed to accept new knowledge and understanding. We all have learning preferences, learning differences and more importantly favourite beliefs about ourselves and our ability that we want to hang on to. Learning is a process of change and development; it's about loosening our grip on a reality we have come to believe in, and embrace uncertainty and the fearful unknown.

Most people are comfortable with accepting new ideas as long as the new doesn't conflict with or challenge existing beliefs and preconceived ideas. When it does we try to use the new to support the old or initially reject it out of hand. Unfortunately, we can't develop and grow and stay where we are at the same time; change is the basis of the learning experience, while certainty requires a sense of permanency and is opposed to change. Knowledge and understanding never comes to us complete so the learning it brings is transitional; and this state of change is the only real constant in life. No matter how stable or fixed a thing may first appear it is in a constant process of transformation.

Nothing ever stays the same indefinitely and our resistance to change comes primarily from a need to feel in control and from a fear of losing something that we have claimed ownership to. If we resist change and fight to stay where we are we can hang on to what makes us feel safe and secure, even if it's no longer valid, an illusion or simply a mistaken belief. We also fear and distrust anything or anyone who appears different to our rigid definition of normal, because different is change by another name, and we fear and distrust what we don't understand be it a person, belief or a new idea. Yet belief is often nothing more than make-believe, a feeling of certainty; we are certain of what we believe and those beliefs provide us with the evidence and proof of our convictions.

If we aren't careful we can box ourselves in by a rigid mindset, a 'box' that we must learn to think outside of, if we wish to find innovation and motivation for change. Few if any of our beliefs are new and original, they are handed down from generation to generation, usually by our parents and adults of influence. In effect, they all took on the role of teachers and we were the blank page upon which their beliefs were laid down, and with a child's innocence and trust we accepted them as our own. We should never blame ourselves or our teachers for the truths we can no longer accept without question, for they could only teach us what they themselves had learnt. But acceptance of the new should never automatically be at the expense of the old; both the new and the tried and tested should be challenged and held to the light of scrutiny, to establish their validity, value, and worth.

Education is healing, and healing is about change; that process can be evolutionary learning from past mistakes, where the new is an extension of the old, and builds on the foundations laid by what has gone before. Or it can be revolutionary in its desire to sweep away the old and replace it with a new set of values and beliefs. In reality, there is nothing new under the sun and what goes around eventually comes around. What exists in the present moment in time is an extension of what was, and will be again, albeit in a different format, it may look different and have a different title but even the new owes its existence to the knowledge and understanding that made it possible. The understanding of one self and recognising the belief based limitations we hold onto and those we see as different, is the first step in being able to understand and appreciate the value of others. In doing so we begin to heal personal, cultural and social differences.

Chapter 5 - You may be spiritual, but are you for real?

When we look to define the word 'authentic' we come up with a number of definitions that can help us understand what an authentic person may look like. To be authentic you must not be a copy, false or an imitation. You will be real; genuine in the way you represent your true nature or beliefs. You will be true to yourself and as such worthy of acceptance for who and what you are.

In spite of the artificial and sometimes illusionary barriers and borders created by politics and religion to keep us segregated for the purpose of manipulation and control, we co-exist on this planet with approximately eight billion other souls who share more similarities than they do differences. They may look like different makes and models, but we all came off the same production line and we all conform to the same genetic blueprint. But with so many people on this planet unless we are sure of our own personal identity it becomes easy to get lost in the crowd; to blend in becomes a greater attraction than the desire to stand out and be recognised as an individual in our own right. There is safety in numbers and security of a shared comfort zone that takes away the pressure of individual thought and action, allowing us to go with the flow, in the belief that we can't all be wrong.

> If we desire to be **authentic** then the first step is to recognise and accept that it's an inside job, an internal journey that we alone can make in order to meet and **get to know this stranger that lives our life**, and eventually reach a point of **self-realisation**.

Authenticity requires a reality check; authenticity can't be verified unless we have the courage and desire to strip away the years of conditioning placed upon us by parents and role models in our formative years, by tradition, social expectation and dogma. Each in their way covers us with a veneer of conformity that eventually hides the true personality within. If we desire to be authentic then the first step is to recognise and accept that it's an inside job, an internal journey that we alone can make in order to meet and get to know this stranger that lives our life, and eventually reach a point of self realisation. It has to be said, this isn't for the faint hearted for as each layer is considered before being retained or discarded our personalised comfort zone shrinks until the only thing left to face is our true self. Self that is stripped back and devoid of pretence, no longer able to hide behind expedient beliefs and values. To authenticate the true self takes both time and effort and in a society that values artificial reality and celebrity status above the truth, it's much easier for some to create the illusion of authenticity by adopting a wide range of in vogue personas.

Off the peg values, beliefs, and opinions that can be mixed and matched to suit all occasions, disguises that become nothing more than another layer that hides the person within. Those who seek to hide their true nature from even their own reflection in the mirror live in fear of the day the mirror loses its power to lie and they see nothing but empty eyes and an empty life reflected back to them. Spirituality doesn't grant special dispensation to those who would look to hide their true personality in the trappings of 'Namaste', nor does it own the monopoly on righteousness. The true nature of spirituality lies not in its name or what we perceive it to be, it's found in even the smallest action expressed it in our daily lives. Some may seek to wear it as a mantle to cover and conceal while others use the light they find within it to uncover their own shadows in an effort to achieve transparency and their authenticity.

Chapter 6 - Oh my God, your Reiki is so last year

A name no matter how descriptive or ''spiritual'' is just a label that we attach to those who look different, behave differently, and have a different faith, belief or culture. The moment we label certain groups or individuals in a less than empowering way we define ourselves more than we do them.

The understanding of differences requires us to look beyond the superficial labels that separate us and find the common ground that we share. Acknowledge and respect the person beneath the many labels, the baggage they have to carry, and the belief based limitations they have to deal with. Intelligence comes in many forms and takes many guises; and comparisons can be painful and self defeating when we judge one persons capacity for learning and personal development against another based on our own beliefs, preconceived ideas and fears.

What is a single step to one person may be a milestone to another; all achievement is relevant to the steps we are able to take, and the personal barriers we have the strength and courage to overcome. We all have learning difficulties and differences to one degree or another; we all have belief based limitations and favourite beliefs that keep us in our comfort zone. We all have blind spots when it comes to seeing things we don't want to face up to and deal with. Learning and personal development isn't about judging ourselves or others harshly for some perceived weakness or deficiency, it's about understanding and developing a willingness to loosen our grip on reality, letting go of old ideas and beliefs that no longer support us, reflect the person we have become or more importantly the person we aspire to be regardless of the labels we wear.

Chapter 7 - My inner child is in here somewhere

Every experience seeks expression. Writing provides a means of communication where, as the author, I can also become the narrator of my life story. When I am unable to speak the words, writing allows the pain of the past to gain recognition and help bring about the closure necessary in order for the present moment to take its rightful place in my life. In telling the story I am able to gain clarity, and when I can recount my story without the shedding of tears I know the healing of that particular chapter in my life is complete.

Writing is a process of self-discovery during which we can bring closure to the past while creating a future we wish to experience. Knowledge and understanding of oneself is the true healer and when we can make peace with our past, like friends we are free to part on good terms.

Chapter 8 - Reiki, hold my beer I've got this

When people first come to Reiki they are often inspired to try and put into words what it felt like when they experienced that rush for the first time. The following was my feeble attempt at trying to convey how it made me feel at the time.

Without knowing your name or understanding why, I searched for you and invited you into my life. Softly you entered and helped bring about changes that left me in awe of your power. Never against my will discover new ways and remember truths learnt many lifetimes ago, with each new opportunity a chance to break new ground and old beliefs in equal measure.

Where my foot falls matters not, for the lessons learned and the truths to be discovered are forever **within.**

Although my destiny is already secure, I must still take each step on my journey that will one day return me to my spiritual home. Where my foot falls matters not, for the lessons learned and the truths to be discovered are forever within. My journey merely provides the experiences necessary to discover them, for my destination is a state of mind that helps me discover my true self and be at one with all things in a universe that created me.

The way of Reiki is a journey we all can take; a journey during which we are both student and teacher, a seeker of truth and the giver of wisdom, each step gifts us the opportunity to find the knowledge and understanding we search for. Weary we may stumble and fall and question our beliefs, but in those times of fear and uncertainty the voices we hear echo the doubts of others seeking guidance on their own journey of discovery.

I was taught Usui Reiki in the traditional way and I accepted everything without question, even when certain things didn't appear to make sense to me or work in the way they were supposed to. These short comings were more than made up for by the euphoric buzz I was getting from what I was studying. Without realising it no matter how disjointed some of the teachings appeared it was serving a very important purpose in my life at that time.

Parts of my life were fractured and broken and Reiki was helping me become aware of the work that was needed to repair and make me a whole person again. Like some disjointed articulated puzzle the inconsistencies in my training began to reflect and mirror my shattered life, yet it brought with it a feeling that the more things were brought together the more they would make sense. Slowly I began to put my life back together piece by piece. In the process Ibegan to question everything about myself in order to get a better understanding of how and why the damaged child had grown into a damaged man full of anger, self-loathing and despair. Like a child building a picture puzzle, I looked for straight edges to provide structure in the form of reasons why, colours and patterns fit together in the shape of cause and effect. Slowly a picture emerged out of the darkness and confusion, and brought with it healing and peace of mind that only deep understanding can give. With understanding comes the desire to know more and so we begin to question the old and the new in equal measure.

A belief tested either validates its teaching or highlights inconsistencies and failings that must be challenged, if not we are simply perpetuating myths and misconceptions for the sake of tradition and expediency. Often an original concept can become corrupted as people look to change and adapt what they themselves were taught to keep pace with current knowledge and understanding and that's how it should be, but if the underlying principles are sound they will remain constant and provide a link that connects the past, present, and future.

Reiki was and is a discipline of personal spiritual development, the only person we have a duty to, and ability to heal is ourselves.

Knowledge and understanding may change but truth remains constant, and when the principle is proven true and correct all that's required on our part is practice and commitment to create the reality we desire.

In Usui's teachings there were three principles that to me underpinned everything he believed and taught. What we call Reiki was and is a discipline of personal spiritual development, the only person we have a duty to, and ability to heal is ourselves. This we are able to through the power of our attention (what we focus on) and our intention, (what we choose to do about it). No matter how much I read and study I keep coming back to these principles, and they form the basis of everything I teach in the form of sixty-week Reiki personal development programme. To me there is no middle ground, Reiki either works or it doesn't. Bullshit no matter how spiritual it appears does nothing more than confuse the gullible and feed on people's ignorance and fear. When it promises miracle cures and short cuts to happiness, both inevitably lead to dead ends and disappointment. Empty promises are a true reflection of character of those that make them, and of a spiritual product that needs to be hyped up to cover its short comings and failings. Reiki is not some kind of magical cleaning product with a new and improved formula that kills 99% of all known germs and does all the hard work so you don't have to. It can work wonders, but its active ingredient is knowledge and understanding and its catalytic power comes from us taking responsibility for our own lives and accepting we have a duty of care to do everything in our power to improve our health and well-being. Life is a team game; we play our part and the conscious healing energy we have labelled Reiki takes care of the game plan that's beyond our level of control. We do what only we can do, and it takes care of the rest in direct relation to the time, effort, and energy we commit to our spiritual development.

Life is a **team game**; we play our part and the conscious healing energy we have labelled Reiki takes care of the game plan that's beyond our level of control.

I have been asked many times what first attracted me to Reiki. The truthful answer is I didn't know at the time or even give it much thought as to what interested me enough to find out what it was. At the time, I was very much into martial arts. I had chosen to study Aikido for the spiritual development aspects of the discipline and I was helping my instructor with some research to see if it was financially viable to set up a centre of excellence in the area. During my research, I came across a poster advertising a Reiki evening and thought it sounded 'martial' and as there was a contact number I gave them a call. We had a lovely and lengthy conversation during which they explained what Reiki was and I was invited to come along and see for myself. I accepted the invitation and that night my life changed in so many ways and the clock began ticking on many aspects of my life that would sooner or later have to come to an end. The evening was relaxed and

49

informal; the small group were very friendly and open but I quickly noticed that the conversation was guarded when the topic of Reiki was raised and this both concerned and intrigued me in equal measure.

My curiosity was engaged but I also made sure my exit route was clear should I need to escape in a hurry. The first sign of chanting, cauldrons or green mist and I would be out of there. Television and the cinema have a lot to answer for but I had nothing to fear other than my own ignorance and fear. It was here that I met the lady who would become my first Reiki Master.

The host asked if anyone would like to have some Reiki and helped us make our way to the treatment room that occupied another part of the house. Two or three treatment beds had been set up, and at this point the Reiki teacher took the lead and the informal session got underway. The room was light and airy with what I would come to consider the obligatory Reiki cosmetics of candles, crystals, and water feature and 'spiritual' background music. Like many new to the discipline I looked around the room and mistakenly thought to myself "so this is what Reiki looks like".

I had a similar thought not so long ago; I was in heavy traffic and noticed a lady standing at a bus stop. It was a cold grey wet day and I instinctively knew she could do with a little Reiki first aid pick me up, so while I waited for the traffic to start moving again I simply used my intention to give her some Reiki. I was in my car devoid of any paraphernalia, there wasn't a candle, crystal or water feature in sight and the only music was the Eagles singing Hotel California on the radio and I thought to myself.... ''so this is what Reiki looks like''.

That first fateful night I got my chance to take my place on one of the treatment beds and I remember the teacher and two or three of her students gently laid their hands on my head and shoulders, chest and lower legs. Any feelings of uncertainty were quickly replaced by a sensation that appeared to start outside of my body, yet I felt 'it' spreading inside and with this feeling of expansion a sense of deep relaxation and heightened euphoria. Although people were quietly talking to me I just wanted everyone to shut up and give me a moment so I could try and rationalise what was happening to me. When I was asked how I felt it was like the spell had been broken and the euphoric relaxation began to ebb away. I wanted to chase after it and try to hang onto it, I was hooked. I remember telling them that I wanted to learn how to do Reiki but more importantly, I needed to learn how to become a Reiki Teacher so that I could help others gain the same kind of insightful awareness that I had just experienced.

If I had realised the price I would have to pay I may have had second thoughts before setting out on that particular part of my journey. That incisive moment of realisation was both the beginning and end. It was the beginning of my Reiki journey but it was also the end of the things in my life that I would need to let go of. Let go of in order that knowledge and understanding could take their place, so that healing of mind body and spirit could be the effect to their cause. This included ill health and disease, my broken and dysfunctional marriage, a job I had grown to hate, and my family and home which had become collateral damage as everything began to fall apart. We always assume that healing equates to the influx of great stuff for our highest good. It does ultimately, but the process of elimination and detox can be a very painful and stressful process to go through. All of the negative and destructive thoughts, beliefs and values begin to either fall away of their own accord or have to be prised from our grasp, as we try to hang onto out of fear, no matter how dangerous or self-debilitating it may be.

I would go on to do my Reiki first and second degree training with my first teacher and it's fair to say that my training was an anti climax compared to the initial experience described above. This was no reflection on the quality of the training I received but solely on my own unrealistic expectation of what my training would achieve for me. Although I did have some meaningful insights that required time and hard work to provide perspective and understanding, I have to say, at the time I was feeling totally unimpressed with what appeared to be unfulfilled promises, and more than a little concerned I had been conned out of my training fees. Before my time with that particular teacher came to an end she took me to one side to discuss my training and the contents of my reflective diary. She made some ''predictions'' as to where she felt my training would lead, my teaching ability and people I would be go on to help. You would think that having your teacher heap praise upon your shoulders and laying out before you the road you will eventually travel would be a marvellous experience. To me it was uncomfortable, and only served to highlight some of the stuff I would have to learn and accept about myself before letting go of baggage I had been carrying for so long. Part of that baggage was very poor self image and low self esteem; I have never been comfortable with compliments because I always feel they are misplaced or undeserved. I have improved with age to the point when paid a compliment I will now accept it and simply say thank you.

Back then was very different; imagine if you will a conversation where an ugly duckling is being helped to see he is a Swan in the making. *"Me a Swan, you're kidding me right, look at this beak, these ugly feathers and my size eleven feet, you're the swan and me...I'm just an ugly duckling'.* Unfortunately, all these years later when I force myself to look in the mirror I still don't see a swan, but the personal development work is paying off. In my eyes, I'm still a duck, but with silver hair and beard, I'm now willing to accept I'm a ''distinguished looking duck''.

Unfortunately, all these years later when I force myself to look in the mirror I still don't see a swan, but the **personal development work** is paying off. In my eyes, I'm still a duck, but with silver hair and beard, I'm now willing to accept I'm a **"distinguished looking duck"**.

That initial contact was in 1999 and now some 18 years later can I answer the question with some confidence based on a lot more knowledge and understanding than I had back then. The energy we refer to as Reiki or as I imagine it to be, Golden White light, made up of three indivisible components. Healing through the acquisition and application of knowledge and understanding, unconditional love that is none judgemental expressed through cause and effect. Last but not least, divine spirit the creative power source that holds everything in place. I have to say that this is just my theory, but it works for me.

Reiki - Golden White light
is made up of 3 indivisible components:
1. **Healing** through the acquisition and application of knowledge and understanding.
2. **Unconditional love** that is none judgemental expressed through cause and effect.
3. **Divine spirit** the creative power source that holds everything in place.

The next step on my Reiki Journey led me to search out and eventually find a Reiki Master who would complete my training allowing me to become an advanced practitioner and Reiki

Master. The search was neither simple nor straight forward but it provided me with the opportunity to get acquainted with some ''Masters'' with large ego's that would only teach me if I was willing to accept their teachings as the one true version of the Reiki story and reject everything I had already learnt. I was offered the chance to become a Master in a day. This person didn't teach as such, but was willing to teach me how to be a Reiki Master in approximately eight hours for the princely sum of £5,000. By my calculations that's an hourly rate of £625, nice work if you can get it. I respectfully declined the offer and travelled nearly 300 miles south to find my teacher living just outside of London.

Tina lived in a cottage literally a stone's throw from the river Thames. She had a beautiful home, great energy and a down to earth no nonsense approach which resonated with me from the outset and our initial telephone conversations. My training lasted three days, it was relaxed and enjoyable, but from a Reiki perspective it left me more than a little underwhelmed and asking myself ''is that it, is that what all the fuss is about''. Six months later I felt ready to start teaching Reiki; unfortunately, it was my ego that was making all the arrangements. Expensive training venue, costly training fees, Chicken buffet lunch, and the surroundings were far more impressive than my teaching ability or the content of the course. Mistakenly I wanted people to associate me and ''my Reiki'' with the trappings of success and I failed miserably; people were able to see me for what I was, a fraud, a wanna be, pretending to be a Reiki Master teacher.

Two things I knew for certain; Reiki worked, I just didn't know how, and I wanted to teach people how to improve their health and well-being by having Reiki in their lives. It quickly dawn on me that a Reiki Master certificate didn't carry any weight at all when it came down to teaching students and I would need to supplement that certificate with real teaching qualifications and hands on experience. If I was going to be a Reiki teacher I was determined to be the best that I could be and I knew that if I did my bit Reiki would take care of itself.

Chapter 9 - Commitment to my own development

That moment of clarity set me on a path of learning and study that continues to this day but back then I didn't realise just how my teaching and Reiki would become so infused it would be impossible to see where one ended and the other began. A copy of my qualifications and training record are included in the appendices at the end of this book.

If Reiki was providing me with a purpose in life, it was a childhood of abuse, neglect and deprivation that was providing the inspiration and direction of my teaching practice. I knew instinctively the people who needed my help the most; they were people in dark places who could relate to my childhood experiences. We shared a common bond and many of the same nightmares so I sought out the training I needed in order to help those who I felt needed me the most. I didn't realise it at the time but working with special needs, abused children and abusive and damaged parents were playing a major part in my own healing process. The commitment to my own personal development and training opened the door to many opportunities that I would normally not have access to. One such opportunity was when I had the chance to teach Reiki personal development in a maximum-security prison as part of their summer activity programme. Over several weeks I worked with the general inmates on a morning, then in the afternoon work with the vulnerable prisoners who were segregated for their own safety. These included murderers sex offenders and paedophiles.

I was lucky enough to work on that programme for two years, during which time I had the chance to take some of my students with me to assist in delivering the programme, and to help them with their training and development. It was both stressful and exhilarating at the same time. I went into that experience with my eyes open but blinkered by the preconceived ideas about what I would find inside those heavily fortified walls. During my short time there all of that was stripped away and I left with a better understanding of myself and human nature. I went in proud of the fact that I had faced my own darkness and survived, but I came face to face with people whose darkness was so black and so deep I couldn't begin to fathom the depth of their despair or try to put myself in their place.

During my time there two inmates left me with lasting memories. One thanked me for giving him his first good night's sleep in the twelve years he had been in there. The second inmate was built like a brick outhouse; he was so big his prison uniform had to be tailored to fit his impressive bulk. He sat at the back of the room never speaking, and on my final day he got up and approached me, which I have to admit scared the crap out of me as the guard was outside in the corridor reading his paper and having a cuppa. This giant of a man gently shook my hand, and in a softly spoken voice thanked me, saying how much he had enjoyed my class. He left the room and I never saw him again. When I enquired who he was, I was informed he was originally from Eastern Europe, had a paramilitary background and was personally responsible for the deaths of an unspecified number of people due to his part in the ethnic cleansing that took place during the military conflict in that area. The thing I remember the most about this man was not his size which was undoubtedly impressive, it was his eyes. Eyes that were so dark they looked pitch black; they lacked warmth and compassion, and appeared empty. Cold and lifeless, a darkness that was fearful, yet the pain they concealed resonated with my own pain that was yet to be healed.

My childhood and that of my brother and sister were destroyed by the effects of mental health issues, drink, drugs, and violence. We came from a broken home and a totally dysfunctional family, our mother was abused as a child and suffered from manic depression and a personality disorder. She was addicted to prescribed medication including Barbiturates and amphetamines amongst many others, and was dependent on alcohol to supplement the effects of the medication. I suffered with depression from an early age and was prescribed Librium and Valium to help cope with the depression and the stress of helping my older brother look after our mother whose behaviour over time was becoming more and more erratic and dangerous to herself and those around her, including us.

She was extremely violent; on one occasion, she was looking after one of her nephews who wasn't very old. They got into a heated argument; he threw something at her hitting her in the face, he then dived under a table to hide and get out of the way. She reached under the table, pulled him out by his hair and then cut his throat with a carving knife. Miraculously he didn't die and many fears later he showed me the scar on his neck and took a great delight in telling me ''that's where your mother cut my throat''.

One of the lasting memories of my childhood was when my mother held a knife to my brother's throat threatening to kill him. I and my younger sister were made to stand to watch obviously there was a lesson to be learnt by all of us. I have no idea what that lesson was, but I can still remember him screaming begging her to stop. When I was eighteen I returned the favour and tried to kill my mother for all that she had done to us. Something saved both of us; saved her life and saved me from spending years in prison for murder. I did however spend a week in a psychiatric unit as a voluntary patient during which time I met fellow patients that scared the crap out of me, inspired me while others made me feel ashamed of wallowing in self-pity and hopelessness. I had no idea then what a pivotal moment in my life this was, it was much later that I recognised it as a blessing in disguise.

Over the years I have worked with many medical and training professionals and the terminology they used to describe various emotional and mental health conditions, but the only one that came close to describing my family and our childhood was we were ''totally fucked up''. Although difficult at the time the experience would be invaluable later in life when I took on the role of carer in a secure psychiatric unit for female patients. It was if my life had turned full circle.

I had gone from being a victim of mental, emotional and psychological abuse as a child, to a carer in a position to help those who needed my help the most. It wasn't plain sailing as I was targeted the whole time by a patient who demonstrated the same symptoms and violent personality that my mother did. Initially I automatically slipped back into the victim mentally which the patient instinctively picked up on. I began to question my ability until a very experienced team leader stepped in and explained that none of it was my stuff, it was the patient's condition that was driving her behaviour and it wasn't personal. I let go of the victim mentality, my attitude changed and I'm proud to say I became very good at my job because I was able to draw on a life time of prior experience that added a different dimension to my relationship with the patients.

After two and a half years I decided the time was right to retire to focus on my writing and putting together my Reiki personal development programme. It was almost like Reiki was saying to me ''Ok Phill enough of the studying, let's see what you have learnt, show me what you have got''. My answer was simple and unequivocal. ''Reiki! Hold my beer, I've got this shit''.

Chapter 10 - Returning to where it all began

In the 1800's around about the same time Usui was sitting up a mountain counting his pebbles and "allegedly" waiting for enlightenment, tiny hamlets and villages were springing up across the north east of England. Their roots were buried deep in the coal seams that gave purpose and meaning to their very existence. I was born in a small rural market town that was once a pit village called Crook.

It first appeared on the map as a tiny agricultural village around 1795 and by 1835 agriculture had given way to a thriving mining industry; this was due to the vast coal seams which lay very close to the surface. Sometimes it would break free to bruise and scar the surrounding landscape as the grass died back to reveal the precious coal beneath. At its height there were over 20 drift mines around the area which led to a rapid growth in the population as people migrated into the area from far and wide to find work and hopefully improve their quality of life and standard of living. However, the prosperity was relatively short lived as by the early 1900's the coal seams began to peter out and the mines and dependant local industries started to close resulting in extreme hardship and poverty. As time went on all that would be left of this once thriving industry was the rusting skeletal remains that dotted the landscape. Eventually be removed for salvage or simply abandoned and overgrown to such an extent it appeared as if the land had waited patiently to reclaim what had been taken from it.

Prosperity came at a very high price; it was a hard and uncompromising life that claimed countless lives. The coal didn't give up without a fight and many miners paid the price with their lives, some died underground in accidents and roof falls, many more died years later from the condition known as black lung disease or miner's pneumoconiosis caused by breathing in the corrosive coal dust.

As the coal dust inevitably found its way into the lungs of the miners, so the hardship of everyday life ate its way into the psyche of those who had to endure it. It broke bodies and spirit in equal measure, stooped over as if weighed down by some invisible burden, their story etched upon weary and worn out faces that aged long before their time. Communities are made by the ties that bind them together, the joy, grief, and sorry felt by one is shared by all and helps form a sense of identity and a pride in their heritage. The courage of those who clawed the coal from the earth's grasp helped forge the character and identity of generations to come, but as always, time commands the final word. Time can heal or it can destroy, and when nothing remains of the past, memories and traditions are only kept alive by those who choose to remember them. Time moves everything on and new generations move further and further away from the past and in doing so new traditions are established and new foundations are set in place on which to build their own future.

Time can heal or it can destroy, and when nothing remains of the past, memories and traditions are only kept alive by those who choose to remember them.

This is how it should be; the sons of the miners who toiled underground followed in their father's footsteps out of necessity, not out of choice. These were men of strength and courage who faced life's hardships on a daily basis because they knew no other way to earn a living. Ordinary men who wanted nothing more than a better life for their families, it was this dream that drove them underground to do dangerous, back breaking work so that generations to come would never have to. If we owe these men a debt of gratitude we should repay them in a way that acknowledges their sacrifice but also fulfils their dreams of a better life for future generations. The village of Chilton in County Durham shares the same story of my home town. Location and place names are different but its history and heritage are one of the same and in many ways interchangeable with their location being the greatest difference. As new building developments and modern housing estates spring up they slowly lose their original identity. As the land inevitably covered and reclaimed the coal fields so modern developments will without realising it, use the past as a foundation for their own future.

Money, wealth, and prosperity provide freedom of choice, but it's knowledge and understanding that empowers us to create the changes we desire, for without it we are victims of fate and circumstances as our ancestors found to their cost. Little did I realise when I was born in Crook all those many years ago, my personal journey and determination to overcome the effects of an abusive childhood would lead me to teach Reiki in the Chilton Community College less than twelve miles away from my birthplace. A short distance geographically, but a lifetime away from my own roots. A childhood that helped forge my inner strength and character, and would eventually fuel my desire to overcome ignorance and fear. I needed to understand what happened to me and more importantly why. I was determined to let go of my victim mentality, reclaim my personal power and become the person I wanted to be. Once I realised knowledge and understanding was the secret, it was only a matter of time before I discovered Reiki was the key to unlocking this personal power and the direction my life would take. More importantly it would lead me to the Community College in Chilton where I would learn my craft, hone my teachings skills in preparation for my return in

January 2017 to develop and deliver my Reiki personal development programme.

Chapter 11 - Don't look to Usui, me or Reiki to live your life for you

Usui made it quite clear to his students, they should not look to him to heal them or live their life for them. It was their life, their responsibility and they must accept the duty of care that went with it. It wasn't his, or Reiki's responsibility to live their life for them. Times have changed but this principle remains as true now as it was then, but human nature being what it is, now more than ever we look for the easier option. That short cut and the quick fix to our problems, but unlike the Matrix film, there isn't a red magic pill, and it's important when we work with Reiki we don't adopt a victim mentality, or look to Reiki as a substitute for common sense, logic and rational thinking. If you are the cause of your problems, then it stands to reason you are the best person to rectify them.

Usui made it quite clear to his students, they should not look to him to **heal** them or **live their life** for them.

This sounds simple, but it's not the game most people want to play, adults with a childlike naive mind set, who don't really want to change. They want to continue doing their own thing, but want someone or something to sort out all the crap for them. They want change, as long as they are the ones who don't have to change in the process.

 Healing and education are brothers from a different mother, the two sides of the same coin; Usui realised through his own experience that the student of study, or the student of life must take responsibility and play an active part in their own healing and learning. He understood that knowledge and understanding are the physicians of health and the teachers of truth. Good health isn't a gift to be given, it's a truth that must be learnt and understood. Gifts although gracious, rarely if ever bring with them a true sense of worth or value in the attainment or achievement of the gift itself. Ignorance and fear are blissfully unaware of the closed mind that holds them captive; good health is taken for granted, its true worth is only appreciated when it begins to fade or is lost forever. Knowledge and understanding have the power to free the mind, and in doing so bring with it an appreciation of the true nature of good health and the role we alone can play. Self-awareness is the greatest gift that we can give to ourselves, for it allows us to

release a victim mentality and recognise our true self-worth, and the creative power within us.

Knowledge and understanding are the physicians of **health** and the teachers of **truth**.

If you promote Reiki as something it's not, then failure is guaranteed. All of the hype and empty promises can't make up for lack of substance, and it will only be a matter of time before reality kicks in as the induced euphoria wears off. It either does what it says on the tin or it's bullshit that serves no other purpose that to perpetuate ignorance and fear. If you believe Reiki is a miracle cure, you are unwittingly making a statement that you are powerless to live your own life and your health and well-being can only be achieved through divine intervention. If on the other hand you step up and take personal responsibility for your own learning and the healing that brings, you quickly realise that Reiki stripped back to its basic components, devoid of the myths, misconceptions, bullshit, and old wives' tales, is simply a discipline of personal spiritual development. This is what Usui envisaged and the basis of my personal development training programme.

Chapter 12 - Living without learning is a total waste of life

As I have already said Chilton community college was where I learnt my craft; through the education in the community programme I was able to hone my teaching skills, and effectively lay the foundation of the programme I deliver to my students today. I now give my time free of charge as a tutor and as a member of the management committee, it's my way of giving something back to the community, it brings revenue into the college and helps them to subsidise the course fees to the students. Level's 1, 2, and 3 are run over ten weeks, and the Master Teacher class is a thirty-week course, with a comprehensive support structure in place to underpin the two hours training sessions.

All students are provided with my contact details which they can use as and when they need to. They can email or message me at any time and I will reply as soon as I can, but if they wish to speak to me directly I make myself available to do so between the hours of 7.00pm and 9.00pm, weekdays. On a weekend, it's as and when they can get hold of me. As their self-confidence and self-reliance grows their need to contact me out of hours decreases to the point where they will only do so if it's absolutely necessary.

Part of the support provided is access to a resource library on my website. This is password protected, only available to my students, as is the group page on Facebook that was set up to encourage students to keep in touch and support one another. The group page also allows me to provide feedback to the students on the way their session went, and their progress as a group. Individual feedback is given on a one to one basis in a way that best suits the student's needs. Students are encouraged to join the group support page, it's not compulsory and the decision is theirs to make. Technical support is also available from Barry Hamilton at Badger Design Studio in Glasgow, Scotland. Barry has worked with me for a number of years and is the guy I go to for advice and guidance on all things technical. We have collaborated on a number of eBooks and his sound, no nonsense down to earth approach resonates perfectly with me.

The levels of training may vary but the format and approach is one that has proven itself to work. Each level has its own set of course notes with an introduction and rationale. Each has a syllabus that covers each week, the topics to be covered, handouts and homework to be completed for the following week. The syllabus provides structure, but is in some ways, an administrative tool as personal development is just that, individual and as such can't be pre-programmed. My students are never pigeon-holed regardless of their background and Reiki personal development training is designed to adapt to the individual student's needs. The age of the students varies from teens to seniors, and I have to be sensitive to the fact that some of the mature students may not have completed formal studies for a number of years, so it's important to me, and a vital part of the programme that all of the classes are relaxed and informal, with fun, laughter and enjoyment high on the agenda. Learning of any description must be fun and laughter is a brilliant way of raising a person's energy, and kick starting their learning and healing process.

Another aspect that is unique to this programme is the way students from one level can sit in on the other classes. There is a set attendance level for all the groups: the Master class is 80% and 75% for the other three levels. This takes into consideration that people have other commitments, and I totally accept that life has a habit of introducing unforeseen problems into the best laid plans. The students are expected to complete the work from the weeks they missed, as well as making up the time if they drop below the set attendance level. To do this they are encouraged to sit in on the other groups to make their time up. If students reach the end of their course and still have time to make up their certificate is withheld until they do so. This practice sends out a clear message that their commitment is a prerequisite and simply turning up when they feel like it and going through the motions is not an option.

The programme is developing and changing all the time, it has to, in order to keep pace with the needs of the students. Often a student will ask a question or raise a topic for discussion that falls outside of the lesson plan for that session. This can lead to a greater level of understanding on a particular subject and a completely new direction in their studies. This could result in some additional research or homework for them, and for me the task of writing a new piece of work that underpins their new found

knowledge and understanding. If a student produces a great piece of research and submits it as their homework, if they are happy to do so, their work then becomes a resource to be used for the benefit of other students on the programme now, and in the future. In this way a level 1 student has the opportunity to potentially assist in the development of the Master teacher students.

The programme attracts people who have trained in other disciplines and this adds another dimension to the mix of life experience, skills and abilities within the groups. A melting pot that brings together people from different backgrounds and belief systems to learn, understand develop and grow. We have Buddhists, Pagans, Wicca, Atheists, Christians and loads of the ''none of the above'', all sat around sharing their wisdom and personal truth, learning from one another. And you know what? It all works. Healing and learning through knowledge and understanding, and the ability to consider other points of view in a non judgemental way is the true nature and healing power of Reiki.

Chapter 13 - Created by the mind; empowered by intention

This is how we learn regardless of what level we are. First we discuss theories, concepts and beliefs, and then we look to see if we can validate them through supporting evidence or personal experience. If not we have to consider if they come under the heading of myth, misconception or just good old fashioned bullshit. When we have a lesson to learn and develop, we do so through the process of discussion and then supportive practice designed to build practical ability and most importantly, underpinning knowledge and understanding.

This way we are always working from a point of strength and within the realms of our own experience. Mistakes are made when we go beyond the limits of our personal experience, knowledge and understanding. Slow steady progress can sometimes be frustrating when we want to learn as much as we can, as quickly as we can, but small measured steps always lead to the greatest improvement and personal development. The syllabus provides form and structure and gives direction. It maps out the underpinning knowledge and understanding that supports the hands-on practice that we do over and over again. Repetition builds confidence and the level of self-belief that takes us beyond the need to repeatedly say to ourselves ''I can do this''. The problem arises when the student's ability begins to outgrow the syllabus. You can hold them back, rewrite the syllabus or come up with another solution to the problem.

This became a real problem. I knew there was no way I was going to restrict their progress, so I began to update the syllabus almost on a weekly basis which resulted in some very confused students. I had to come up with a better solution to what was becoming a real headache, and the solution was a lot simpler than I first thought. The first step was to get the syllabuses how I wanted them, and then leave them alone, resisting the urge to tweak them further. Then I turned my attention to the sessions themselves. The two hour session was split in half by a short refreshment break so I decided to use that as a means of changing the lesson format. The first half of the session would be given over to covering the syllabus and general Reiki practice, after the break we would move on to practicing various advanced techniques designed to substantiate their underpinning knowledge, develop their sensitivity and energetic awareness, and instill a solid understanding of the concept ''energy follows intent''.

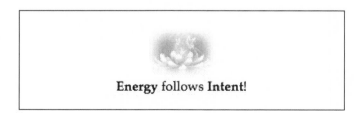

Energy follows **Intent!**

These techniques are now part of the training programme, practiced on a weekly basis throughout their training by all of the students from level 1 to Reiki Master Level. This list is by no means definitive; as students reach a level of competency new exercises need to be introduced to further test their ability, knowledge and understanding.

- Scanning: close up and at a distance using their hands, and then just their eyes
- Bowl of water: blind test, sensing another person's residual energy in the water
- Tray of sand: blind test, sensing another person's residual energy in the sand
- Energy circle: creating a group energy circuit then directing it towards other students
- Line up: moving people without touching them
- Projecting energy over distances of 45 feet and moving people in the process
- Passing an energy ball in a circle from one person to another
- Sensing a person's energy: blind test identifying people behind them by their energy
- Group practice: moving a static object, folded card/ping pong ball/suspended crystal
- Psychometry: reading inanimate objects
- Using imagination to set up Reiki Direct Debits
- Colour therapy: blind test, sensing colour by touch
- Picture profiling: reading a person's photograph

- Dowsing

These exercises, syllabus, and course notes you are about to read provide structure and underpinning knowledge. The above exercises provide the student with the opportunity to have fun, stretch their imagination, improve their sensitivity, develop their skills and gain experiential understanding of energy following their intent. Together they form the basis of my Reiki personal development programme, but unlike rigid tradition this is a live document, a programme that is responsive to the students' needs and able to change to incorporate new and current thinking on personal development, self-healing, and all things Reiki.

Chapter 14 - Reiki Personal Development Programme First Degree

Reiki Level 1

Foreword

The written word provides information; experience provides us with the opportunity to gain knowledge and understanding. As you begin this course you should be aware that *what you are about to read will not enable you to do Reiki.* Reading all of the Reiki books ever written will not make you into a Reiki practitioner; the written word can only provide a backdrop against which hands on experience is viewed. It's the role of any teacher to create a learning environment where by the student can move from the idea and into the experience, encouraging you how to think, but *not* what to think as you take responsibility for your own learning.

This course will provide you with a wealth of information that will build a framework for your Reiki training, personal development and self-healing. Within that framework we will create the opportunity for you to demonstrate your newfound ability and to receive feedback and encouragement as your learning experience progresses. With it will come a better understanding of the ability you have begun to develop. We are facilitators, and channels through which it flows, we don't own it, *but we do have a duty of care and a responsibility to use it wisely.*

An overview of your Reiki Level 1 Course

There is a great deal of information written about Reiki; while a lot of it is educational and informative, some of it is contradictory and this can be very confusing to a student coming to Reiki for the first time. Time and effort is being committed worldwide to discovering the truth about the history of Reiki, who did what, who said what, where and when. This becomes part of the Reiki story because that is all history is, one person or group's account of what may or may not have happened in the past. History is created in the here and now and by choosing to learn Reiki you have become a part of the Reiki story.

The best piece of advice I can give you in regards to all of this debate about the validity of eastern or western Reiki is to not get involved with it, and accept that right and wrong is just *different* by another name. Allow those who wish to argue to do so, and put your time and energy to the best possible use, which is your Reiki practice and personal development.

Accept that **right** and **wrong** is just different by another name.

The Reiki you will learn on this course is a development of both eastern and western styles of Reiki. The western approach is more structured and regimented with somewhat rigid guidelines that tell us what to do and when to do it. *It all works* but I have always found must do's very restrictive, especially when it comes to personal development. I find the esoteric eastern Reiki far more liberating and responsive to the development of those who have come in contact with it.

I have found from my own experience and that of my senior students and Reiki Masters; the more esoteric eastern Reiki allows them far more freedom to discover their own boundaries and then move beyond them. Through knowledge and understanding Reiki has the ability to bring about a healing experience in anyone it comes in contact with if that's what they want, *if they don't it won't* it's as simple as that. This is because healing of any kind comes from knowledge and understanding and requires your participation for it to work; you are the only one that can do this because you are the catalyst that allows the healing process to begin.

Self-knowledge is the first part of the healing process, and the first step on the journey of self-fulfillment. You will be given a series of course notes that will help you understand the healing process and then develop at your own pace, each piece of work has been produced to answer certain questions you may have, but also to stimulate you to ask further questions of me and of yourself.

Over the period of your studies you will develop many new skills and abilities and be given the opportunity to prove to yourself that they really work.

Healing of any kind comes from knowledge and understanding and requires **your participation** for it to work.

Your Reiki Level 1 training programme is a ten-week course consisting of ten two hour training sessions, with the option of on-line support and guidance if and when you need it. Attendance of 75% is required if you wish to receive your certificate of training at the end of the course. Your course notes will include a syllabus that identifies the subjects to be covered over the duration of the course. The syllabus is more administration than education as; *your development can't be predetermined before your course starts,* this is no more than an indication of the direction your training will take, a foundation upon which to build your development, but this will be up to you as like anything else in life the rewards are in direct relation to the effort. Please don't expect to know all there is to know about Reiki by the end of this course, if you do I guarantee you will be disappointed.

If I have done my job properly you will have got to the end of the course and have more questions than answers. Not everyone goes on to be a Reiki practitioner and a smaller percentage decide to continue their training and go on to be Reiki Masters. Either way whatever you decide as far as your training is concerned will be the right decision for you to make. You will have the gift of Reiki at your fingertips for the rest of your life, just waiting for you to use it.

How often you use it and the level of training you achieve will depend on where you are in your life and your need and desire to move forward or not as the case may be. Part of moving forward requires us to occasionally look back to see how far we have come and how we have developed, and from a Reiki point of view that's what I want you to do now. Please remember that the past no matter how good or bad should only be a point of reference and we should never live there. Having looked at the past to gain a baseline or point of reference, we can begin to move forward. Your point of reference is provided by Reiki coming into your life, and this can if you wish, be the benchmark by which you measure your development from this point on.

The **past** no matter how good or bad should only be a **point of reference** and we should never live there.

Reiki Lineage

The following shows your connection to Dr Usui through his successors and the masters they trained. Through this lineage you are able to trace your heritage directly to Dr Usui himself.

Dr. Mikao Usui - The Founder of Reiki

1865-1926

Dr. Chujiro Hayashi - Dr Usui's successor

1878-1940

Mrs Hawayo Takata - Appointed Grand Master by Dr. Hayashi

1900-1980

The Twenty-one Reiki Masters Trained by Mrs. Takata

1970-1980

George Araki, Barbara McCullough, Beth Gray, Ursula Baylow, Paul Mitchell, Iris Ishikura, Fran Brown, Barbara Weber Ray, Ethel Lombardi, Wanja Twan, Virginia Samdahl, Phyllis Lei Furumoto, Dorothy Bada, Mary McFadyen, John Gray, Rick Bockner, Bethel Phagh, Harry Kuboi, Patricia Ewing, Shinobu Saito, Barbara Brown.

You're Lineage through: -	You're Lineage through: -
Iris Ishikura	Phyllis Lei Furumoto
	William
Arthur Robertson	Rand
Karen Cameron	Allan Sweeney
Mary Mooney	Tina Reibl
Allison Agius	Phillip Hawkins
Phillip Hawkins	

Reiki Personal Development programme

Level 1

Course syllabus

WK 1 Introduction to Reiki: what it is, what it isn't, history and tradition

Students prior experiences of Reiki, discuss with group.

Give out course notes and discuss content.

Explain what can stop Reiki working.

Give Reiju empowerments and discuss process and effects on students.

- *Handout: Reiki what it is; and what it isn't*

WK 2 Students experiences Q&A

Students to learn and practice headache technique (cause and effect)

Practice feeling peoples energy field/ aura, playing with energy.

Discuss the setting up of the students "Reflective Diary".

Reiju empowerments

- *Handout: Reiki is too important to be serious*

WK 3 Students experiences Q&A.

Understand the meaning of formless Reiki (moving beyond personal limitations).

Free style treatments, hands on, hands off, and using finger tips only.

Learn the difference between effort and intent.

Reiju empowerments

- *Handout: Limitations of Reiki*

WK 4 Students experiences Q&A

Practice hand positions, seated treatments.

Discuss fear and regret and effect of negative emotions.

Look at how our beliefs create our realities.

Reiju empowerments

- *Handout: Dealing with trauma*

WK 5   Students experiences Q&A

Discuss Chakra's and their relationship to Reiki.

Visualisation techniques, filling auras with colours.

Practice balancing your own Chakra's.

Use of empowered images to begin healing process.

Reiju empowerments

- *Handout: The only person we can heal is ourselves*

WK 6   Students experiences Q&A

Look at different ways of using Reiki: Reiki first aid, as opposed to a Reiki treatment.

Practice and discuss establishing own "style" of giving Reiki.

Discuss concept of Reiki going through 'solid objects'.

Reiju empowerments

- *Handout: Healing energy at your fingertip*

WK 7   Students experiences Q&A

Ways of strengthening your Reiki through use, empowerments and meditation.

Practice moving people without touching them, moving and sensing energy.

Formless Reiki, giving treatments and getting feedback on your progress.

Reiju empowerments

- *Handout: The healing power of happiness*

WK 8 Students experiences Q&A

Discuss the practicalities of distance healing. Myths and misconceptions.

Practice distance healing in pairs and as a group.

Progress on students' reflective diaries.

Reiju empowerments

- *Handout: Looking beyond what we can see.*

WK 9 Students experiences Q&A

Discuss and practice meditation techniques.

Practice and discuss with group progress in own style of treatments.

Discuss the concept of advanced forms of self-healing.

Reiju empowerments

- *Handout: What we believe Reiki to be, is nothing more than an assumption.*

WK 10 Students experiences Q&A

Recap previous weeks of the course and answer any questions.

Discuss the aims and objectives of Reiki Level 2

Student progression on to next level of training

Final Reiju empowerments of Reiki Level 1 course

- *Handout: Reiki before it was Reiki*

If you have reached this point you will have successfully completed your Reiki Level 1 course. I hope you have enjoyed the experience, and have begun to learn something of the mysteries of Reiki. If I have done my job properly I will have answered some of your questions, but given you a lot more to think about in the process. Reiki is no different from anything else in life, what you get out of it is always in relation to the time, thought and effort you are prepared to invest into it and your own personal development. Reiki doesn't create miracles people do; *'If you want something different in your life, you have to do something different'*.

If you feel that you have gone as far as you can or want to at this moment in time, then remember the gift you have at your fingertips whenever you need it. Use it well, use it wisely, keep it real, but above all else keep it fun. If you have enjoyed the course and you want to know more about Reiki, then the Reiki Level 2 course will not disappoint as your journey of personal development continues.

If you want something **different** in your life, you have to do something **different**.

Chapter 15 - Reiki Personal Development Programme Second Degree

Level 2 Course Notes

Foreword

If we were to define Reiki Level 2 or second degree Reiki to give it its traditional title, it would be that level 2 is about symbols, and their use in sending distance healing. My students are taught the traditional concept with the symbols and their use, and then taught the contemporary reality that Usui wasn't big on symbols and preferred the power of intention to move energy around and send it over distances. Let me make it very clear: symbols can work, but not for the reason we think. Symbols are neither magical nor mystical and the only thing that comes close to these two definitions is the personal power of our own intention. Symbols work through the power of our intention; we create them and then empower them, not the other way around. A symbol of a smiley face works just as well as the power symbol or any of the Reiki symbols, and has been tried and tested time and time again.

Symbols work through the power of our **intention**; we create them and then empower them, not the other way around.

The traditional attunement or empowerment procedures can when documented, cover two sides of A4 paper. Or it can, as I have demonstrated to my students on countless occasions, be reduced to the size of a small business card that simply says, ''you can now do Reiki''. The card is handed to the student, who then demonstrates that the energy is flowing through them. What is created by the mind is empowered by our intention. The concept that energy follows intent is a proven reality, and once it is established as a fact all that is required is practice to create the reality we desire. Energy following intent is the foundation upon which everything that follows is built upon. It is formless and free flowing just as Usui said it should be. Please keep this in the forefront of your mind when you read the following course notes.

You have completed your Reiki Level I course with either myself or another Reiki Master, and you feel ready to move forward and achieve Reiki II. In doing so you should be certain, in your own mind, that you understand the principles and precepts of Reiki, the way in which it is used through the power of your intention and the nature of its energetic power. We shouldn't think of Reiki 2 as a large step to take, an obstacle to overcome or to reach a certain level, rather we should look at it as a further development in the process that has already begun within us. Much is made of the need to keep Reiki and its symbols secret and sacred from all of those not trained or attuned to Reiki 2 level, and in doing so, a great deal of confusion is created. We use the words out of context or without realising their original or true meaning. I believe that words such as secret and sacred can lead to confusion and create an atmosphere of mystery which is unnecessary and counterproductive. Reiki transcends all religions and dogma yet we use words like sacred, which are loaded with religious connotations, secret infers knowledge known by only a few, yet the principle of Reiki is that it is an inherent gift available to us all. Respect or reverence could both be used to convey this attitude and approach to Reiki.

It's right that we should be careful about what we discuss with people who don't have an understanding of Reiki, not because it is secret, but because in discussing matters beyond their comprehension and experience, we place them in a situation whereby their knowledge and self-esteem is questioned by their inability to understand. We also run the risk of ridicule by others for discussing in a matter of fact way, a subject that appears unbelievable and far-fetched to the uninitiated.

The principle of Reiki is that it is an inherent gift available to us all.

The creative process in all things, is thought, word, action; in this way all things are made. Thought is the initial creative force, a high vibrational energetic force; the spoken word reduces this energetic frequency, and brings it closer to the physical plane. Finally, our actions bring about the physical manifestation of the energetic concept. Before we can build with our hands, we must first build with our minds. The value of any gift is to recognise its uniqueness and true worth and in showing judgment and discretion. We recognise the true worth of the gift we've been given for the benefit of others and ourselves, and in doing so we show respect and reverence to Reiki, its traditions and those who have gone before us.

Introduction

Before we progress onto level 2 let us look back and clarify three important facts about 'Reiki' and its application.

- Firstly, Dr Usui's system wasn't called Reiki.
- Secondly, his system was never about treating people,
- And finally, his system didn't use symbols.

Usui's System wasn't called Reiki;

Usui's system had no name. Usui referred to the system as either 'his system' or a 'method to achieve personal perfection/development'. His students used the term 'Usui

Do'/Usui Teate meaning hand healing. The name 'Reiki' came later, and may have been used first when the Usui Reiki Ryoho Gakkai was set up after Usui's death. In Japanese the word Reiki is pronounced "Lay-key".

Usui's System wasn't about treating people;

The purpose of Usui's method was personal development, to achieve satori, to find one's spiritual path, and through this heal oneself. Treating others was not emphasised or focused upon, if anything it was simply a side effect.

Not all students were taught the same way, some were taught hand positions when treating the physical body, but others weren't. The approach was intuitive based on the personal development of the student; hand-positions were considered a 'teaching aid'. Students were expected to treat intuitively over whatever period was appropriate. This required a balancing of the person's mind, body and spirit in order to identify and rectify the underlying cause. Once the initial connection was made it was the intention that led to the necessary changes taking place.

Usui's System didn't use symbols;

The vast majority of Usui Sensei's students didn't use symbols. They were never taught to use symbols, neither were they attuned to symbols. The Reiki symbols we recognise as Level 2 symbols were later introduced as a teaching aid, a point of focus to enable students to picture the energies in their minds eye. Other students simply used meditation or mantras as a focal point.

The development of symbolism

Before man learned to speak words and draw letters, he used different drawings and pictures to communicate stories and narratives. Drawings or pictures were used to convey messages and ideas, and symbols were born. Through time, people of all cultures have used symbols to mean many different things; they are an easy way to define an ideology, express an abstract concept or even to denote a group or community identity.

Reiki Symbols
Origins and Meanings

Reiki symbols are shrouded in mystery and owe their origins to ancient wisdom knowledge and understanding. Because of the nature of these symbols their interpretation over the centuries has led to some confusion as to their true meaning, lost or misinterpreted in the process of trying to translate 'eastern concepts into western words'. In the west words in general have well defined meanings, clear definitions and the context in which they are used. In the east and in particular Japan, words have many meanings with single words covering a multitude of concepts. The word **Qi** in Chinese or **Ki** in Japanese has at least 28 different meanings. It's from this point of ambiguity and uncertainty that we struggle to learn and understand.

Chu Ko Rei

Pronounced: Cho Koo Ray

Known as the 'Power Symbol' that can be used by itself or in conjunction with the other symbols. Used by itself this symbol focuses and intensifies Reiki energy, when used with the other symbols it acts as a catalyst to energise and empower them.

The Chu Ko Rei spiral can be depicted as a line drawing connecting the seven main Chakra points, or as a spiral that draws the Reiki energy to a single centre point. There are many cultures and disciplines, Shintoism, Shingon, Tendai Buddhism, that have their own interpretation and definition of this symbol. Japanese culture associate Chu Ko Rei as a 'Divine Decree', while the Shintoism Chu Ko Rei is an order or command that carries with it the right of authority tempered by respect and responsibility.

Sei He Ki

Pronounced: Say Hay Key

This symbol is found extensively in Japan, India, and Tibet. The symbol used in Reiki is a Japanese line drawing of a letter from the Sanskrit alphabet with the effect of producing a mental overhaul. This symbol is based on the trinity of love, light, and power. The Usui Master symbol Dai Ko Myo also reflects and represents these principles and can be found in the Kurama temple scriptures.

Hon Sha Ze Sho Nen

Pronounced: Hone Shah Zay Show Nen

This symbol is a ''composite'' made up from a series of Kanji or Japanese characters. The difficulty arises in trying to understand how the original symbol was used. Each Kanji has many meanings and when various combinations are used they can mean a number of different things. The Japanese Kanji used for Hon Sha Ze Sho Nen is much longer than the one used in Reiki because Kanji of a similar nature have been joined together. The bottom of one character is similar to the top of the following one. This effect is not accidental; it is an established practice to jam characters together to form an energetic effect.

Accepting the limitations of our own language the task is made even harder when we try to unravel the meaning of intricate symbols that convey complex ideals. We struggle to convey these ideals using words that don't exist in our own vocabulary. Much has been learnt recently and research continues in order that we may gain a greater understanding of this symbolism. At level 2 you became a stronger channel for Reiki receiving Reiju empowerments on a regular basis, and by practising intention based energy exercises. Reiju continually reinforces your connection to the source and helps you to grow spiritually.

Second Degree Reiki Guide Lines

This is a level of instruction that introduces the concept of symbolism into your Reiki practice, with the additional emphasis on codes of conduct, practice legal requirements and administration. At this level you will be taught a series of Reiki symbols and shown how to use them through the power of your intention to enhance your Reiki sessions. Their origins, meaning and application are explained in detail, so you get a better understanding of how and why they are used.

Trained to this level, you may feel drawn to become a registered practitioner, if so you will receive the necessary advice and guidance in order for you to fulfill all of the social, legal, medical and administrative criteria in setting up a Reiki practice. Students trained to this level 'can' begin to develop a greater understanding and awareness of the principles of energy and its relation to time, space and its effects on the physical, mental, emotional, and spiritual level.

Preparation for Reiki Second Degree Course

Review your Reiki I course notes on a regular basis. Don't forget what you learned during your Reiki I course. Your self-determination has helped you to get this far, but remember that all healing work is for the higher good of the recipient. Healers are educators, be ready and willing to set aside your own ego and personal will when it comes to what is best for the recipient and accept that you may not have the answers they are looking for. Unless you are medically trained and qualified to do so, never diagnose, prescribe treatment or medication, or psycho-analyse. Always stay within your own training and experience, if in any doubt, refer them to their own doctor. Always respect the privacy and wishes of the recipient without compromising yourself as a Reiki practitioner. You have been given a great responsibility of trust and it is important to keep all client information confidential.

Review your Reiki II course notes on a regular basis along with your Reiki I, no matter how many times you have to read them, there is still a wealth of knowledge for you to discover. Remember that you are receiving a powerful gift that demands self-discipline and respect. Real power is always measured and controlled, its use considered and appropriate. Use it freely, use it well, but always use it wisely, it will provide you with experiences beyond your wildest dreams.

Level 2

Course Syllabus

WK1. Student's experiences from last course Q&A

Course notes, aims and objectives of Reiki 2 course

Progression of the student's reflective diary

The nature of symbology: they provide direction and a point of focus

Discuss the concept of distance healing: energy follows intent/ Reiki Direct Debit/ Proxy

Introduce Reiki Power symbol and practice on white board

Reiju empowerments: physical expression and using intent

Handout: Dr Bollocks Elixir of life

Homework: Research symbols used in other non-Reiki disciplines

WK2. Student's experiences Q&A

Recap on last session, discuss last week's homework

Introduction of the smiley face symbol and practice on white board

Reiki second symbol and practice on white board

Discuss the power of the spoken word: the positive and negative effects (Mantra's)

Introduction to variations of Reiju meditation

Reiju empowerments

Handout: Exactly what is healing?

Homework: Research meditation and how it works

Wk3. Student's experiences Q&A

Recap on last week's session, discuss homework

Introduction of Reiki distance symbol and practice on white board

Discuss origins of this symbol: (Kanji)

Group practice Reiju meditation

Reiju empowerments

Handout: Reiki Direct Debit

Homework: What is ESP?

Wk4. Student's experiences Q&A

Recap on last week's session, discuss homework

Discuss the concept of "Reiki First Aid" as opposed to a standard Reiki treatment

Diagram of hand positions on self and others

Keeping your Reiki practice simple and uncluttered

Why simply holding hands is a very powerful way to give Reiki

Reiju empowerments

*Handout: **Fun is too important to be taken seriously***

Homework: Research what "Traditional" means

Wk5. Student's experiences Q&A

Recap on last week's session, discuss homework

Introduction of proxies into your Reiki practice

Look at different ways of using intention when giving Reiki (visualisation)

What is intuitive guidance, and how can it assist your practice

Reiju empowerments

Handout: Basic Chakra system

Homework: Research what is Intuitive guidance

Wk6. Student's experiences Q&A

Recap on last week's session, discuss homework

Traditional versus contemporary approach to Reiki

Intuitive guidance: look at ways of developing this skill using imagination

Unconditional Reiki: helping those who need it the most, those you like and dislike

Reiju empowerments

Handout: The keys to developing your intuitive guidance

Homework: Send Reiki to someone you like, and to someone you don't like

Wk7. Student's experiences Q&A

Recap on last week's session, discuss homework

Check the progress of reflective diaries

Further development of your style of hands on, hands off, and distance energy work

Discuss various other faiths and belief systems

Simple meditation techniques: finding what works for you

Reiju empowerments

Handout: Attention and Intention

Homework: Find a meditation technique that feels right to you

Wk8. Student's experiences Q&A

Recap on last week's session, discuss homework

Recap information covered on previous weeks

Revisit and discuss any areas of concern or confusion

Introduction to the process of becoming a Reiki practitioner

Reiju empowerments

Handout: Beliefs can't stand alone

Homework: Research requirements of being a Reiki practitioner (business)

Wk9. Student's experiences from last week Q&A

Discuss the implications of becoming a Reiki practitioner

Legal, H&S, administrative and logistic requirements

Discuss any areas of confusion or concern

Reiju empowerments

Handout: Change always creates resistance

WK10. Student's experiences Q&A

Ensure reflective diaries are up to date

Recap and look at individual's development and progress

Discuss progression on to Reiki level 3 course, course outline and syllabus

Final Reiju empowerments

Handout: Creating good health, and good stuff in life

Having completed your Reiki Level 2 course, some will already be preparing yourselves to  continue your training to Reiki 3 and beyond, while some of you may feel that you have gone as far as you can at this moment in time. Whatever you decide is ok, for only you can decide on the speed and direction of your own development. As you come to the end of this particular course please remember that the symbols you have learnt are teaching aids to get you to the point of directed intent, they were never meant to become restrictive or crutches to support you or your Reiki. Learn them, use them if you feel the need to, but don't become restricted by them, and move beyond the symbols into the powerful realms of intention.

The Reiki Level 3 course is designed as a bridging course to help you achieve a much higher level of personal awareness. The aim of this course is to help you to understand what being a Reiki Master entails, and the responsibility that comes with it. At the end of this course you will know if you have the desire and commitment to complete the 30-week Reiki Master training programme. Whatever you decide will be the right decision for you, either way, the course will have helped you understand yourself better, and make a more informed decision about your future development. Whatever you decide the course will have achieved its aims and objectives, which is to get you to understand what it really means to be a Reiki Master, and to decide whether that particular path is for you.

Chapter 16 - Reiki Personal Development Programme Third Degree

Level 3

Advanced Practitioner

The level 3 advanced practitioner course is in effect a bridge that helps the student make the transition from the foundation studies of levels 1 & 2 and the Master Teacher course. It builds on the practice and principles learnt at the lower levels, while introducing new ideas and concepts developed and studied in greater detail at Master Teacher level.

The Chakra system provides an excellent analogy of the position of importance the advance practitioner training holds within the training programme. In the Chakra system, the Heart chakra plays a pivotal role in the control and movement of the body's energy linking the lower three ''physical'' chakra's with the energy of the higher three spiritual chakras. If the lower levels of Reiki are the foundation upon which the Master Teacher course sits, then the advanced practitioner level is the knowledge and understanding that unites it, and bonds it together.

At this level the voice of the spiritual teacher and the scientist are brought together in unison and in harmony. We begin to realise what appears as opposing beliefs are nothing more than misunderstandings brought about by the use of different languages to discuss the same subject. Mankind's quest to understand its own spirituality is the same journey of the physicist that struggles to grasp the truth of quantum entanglement. We are all connected and our journey of enlightenment is one and the same; the paths may vary and the roads that lead us to knowledge and understanding may diverge, but they all serve the same purpose and none stands higher in the presence of the universe that created us.

We are all connected and our journey of enlightenment is one and the same.

When the principle is proven correct all that remains is our practice to create the reality we desire.

Level 3

Course Syllabus

Wk1. Introduction to course aims and objectives

Discuss course syllabus and handouts

Reflect on personal changes as a result of completing levels 1 & 2

Progression from level 2 and relevance of heart based emotions at level 3

Reiju empowerments

Handouts: The true nature of miracles/ Synesthesia/ Blind Reading

WK2. Student's experiences Q&A

Recap on last session, discuss handout

The use of heart based emotions in creating your chosen reality

The difference between a ''want'' and a "need''

Creating only what we want, by knowing what we want and how to get it

Reiju empowerments

Handouts: As I think, so I become/ self-imposed barriers to creation

WK3. Student's experiences Q&A

Recap on last session; discuss handout and student's beliefs/perceptions.

Develop further the concept of Reiki first aid

How Reiki expresses itself through our thoughts and actions

Reiju empowerments

Handout: Thoughts from the stillness

WK4. Student's experiences Q&A

Recap on last session, discuss handout

Uncluttering our Reiki and life, physically doing less, but achieving more

Practice distance/remote scanning and healing

Understand the connection between all things and everyone

Letting go of the need to judge self and others

Reiju empowerments

Handouts: One mind, seven bodies/ scanning the physical body

Wk5. Student's experiences Q&A

Recap on last session, discuss handout

Discuss the concept of forgiveness and its link to illness and disease

How emotion colours and affects our judgment

Chakra imagery and coloured material

Reiju empowerment

Handout: Colour Psychology

Wk6. Student's experiences Q&A

Recap on last session, discuss handout

The power of the spoken word in directing your intention, good and bad

Learning the earth's vibration/language

Practice ''four hands'' heart based technique.

Reiju empowerments

Handout: How sounds affect us, physically, mentally and emotionally

Wk7. Student's experiences Q&A

Recap on last session, discuss handout

Discuss a new and deeper understanding of the 5 Reiki principles.

Changes in perception that may have occurred during course

How knowledge and understanding can raise our ''energetic'' level of awareness

Learning to speak the language of energy and spirit

Reiju empowerments

Handout: The earth's heartbeat is 432

Wk8. Student's experiences Q&A

Recap on last session, discuss handout

Recap on previous weeks and topics covered.

Review learning from all three levels

Discuss possible progression on to the Reiki Master Teacher course

Reiju empowerments

Handout: Is 528 Hz a magic healing number?

Wk9. Student's experiences Q&A

Recap on last session, discuss handout

Who in their right mind would want to become a Reiki Master Teacher?

The difference between a teacher, a healer, and a rescuer and a fraud

Understanding Masters are created by failures not titles or certificates of attendance

Reiju empowerments

Handout: What we think to be true, and believe to be real

Wk10. Student's experiences Q&A

Discuss the content and personal development aims of the Master/Teacher course

No blue or red pills, only commitment and hard work.

Are you worth the commitment to your personal development?

Changing the reflective diary to Master portfolio

Reiju empowerment

Handout: **Energy; that's all there is**

    If you have trained with me from your introduction to Reiki, you will have just completed thirty weeks of training, and I'm sure you will be aware of the changes that have happened in your life during that time. You are now faced with a decision as to whether to continue with your training, and go on to become a Reiki Master Teacher.

    If it's a struggle to make that decision, then you are not yet ready to make what is a big commitment to your own future. When you are ready, the decision will make itself, it will be effortless and appear and feel most natural thing for you to do. There should be no pressure involved in this decision, from you or anyone else; you must do what is right for you, when the time is right to do so.

Being a Reiki Master doesn't mean you have to become a Reiki teacher, you can be a Reiki Master for no other reason than to experience and enjoy this knowledge and understanding in your life. Whatever you choose be gentle with yourself, and take the time necessary to enjoy the journey and the experience, just by being who you are and coming this far, you have made a difference in the lives of so many people, and the world is a better place for you being here.

Just by being who you are and coming this far, you have made a difference in the lives of so many people, and the **world is a better place** for you being here.

Chapter 17 - Reiki Personal Development Programme - Reiki Master Teacher Course

''The greatest challenge we face is to Master ourselves''

Foreword

''When the student seeks to become the Master''

Every lesson in life has a point of reference that answers the question why. Why am I doing this and what is the lesson I need to learn from the experience. A point of reference gives us a starting point and a direction, it becomes a motivational compass when we ask ourselves ''am I headed in the right direction and doing what I need to do in order to achieve my goal''. Without a point of reference, we will simply drift through life at the mercy of currents created by chance and circumstance, moved and motivated by the actions and attitude of others.

When I teach Reiki Masters as part of my Reiki personal development programme my point of reference is the design and implementation of a training programme that will inspire and empower each and every one of my Master students. Inspire them to take ownership of their learning and accept the duty of care for their own lives. Step by step; building their personal experience and raising their level of awareness, whilst underpinning their development with a solid foundation of theoretical and experiential knowledge and understanding. It's not enough to simply provide them with "interesting" spiritual and scientific facts and sound bites, every part of the 30-week course must be able to validate itself and earn its place in the syllabus.

Much like the students who must earn their place on the Master course by their commitment to their studies, the desire to be the best they can be, and drive to improve their health and well-being and heal themselves through the acquisition and application of knowledge and understanding of life and of themselves. The aim is not to try and master Reiki but to master oneself.

The aim is not to try and master Reiki but to master oneself.

Negative ego drives us to know and understand everything straight away in the mistaken belief that knowing something is the same as understanding it. Ego is impatient because it knows its time is limited once the journey of self-development has begun and it seeks to use the collection of information and data as a distraction from the search for spiritual truth, and the ultimate freedom from the ego itself. Seeds sown early in their studies will only come to fruition at the right time, concepts and theories proven correct will only really make sense once practice and the underpinning knowledge and understanding are in place, and all have been thoroughly tried and tested time and time again.

There are no shortcuts, there are no miracle solutions or cures, only steady progress built on a solid foundation of personal experience where the student finds their own point of reference in their life and is able to honestly say *"this is true and I have proven to myself it works"*. As a Reiki Master Teacher, my point of reference must be; am I teaching my students the ability when applied through study and personal practice, the power to change their lives in a positive way. Has it the power to improve their health and well-being in mind, body and spirit, and create for themselves a life they wish to live, not escape from. Only time will tell, for as the student becomes the Master, the quality of their teaching becomes a new point of reference and validation of what was, what is and what will be.

Introduction

Before we begin I need to clarify that the training course you are about to undertake is that of Reiki Master Teacher. Although I have completed all of the necessary training that would entitle me to call myself a ''Master'' I choose not to do so. I am first and foremost a teacher trainer and committed student, the title of Master is one piece of baggage I have no desire to carry. This is a personal choice that should not influence your own decision when it comes to such matters; you must try to be true to yourself at all times.

You must try to be **true to yourself** at all times.

You are about to continue the journey of personal development. You may have completed your preliminary training with me or another Reiki Master, or you may have already qualified as a Reiki Master and simply want to add another dimension to your own teaching by considering other perspectives to the Reiki principles and teaching practices. I'm sure you will have arrived at this point with some idea of what being a Reiki Master Teacher involves, but I'm also sure this will change as you progress through your training. This is how it should be; the change in your beliefs and values is an indication of your ongoing development and personal growth. We must remember that development requires change on many levels, you can't develop yet remain unchanged, change is the process that enables growth and provides the environment for new ideas to be sown in a fertile mind.

All training must reflect that principle through its own ongoing development as new information, knowledge and understanding becomes available. If it doesn't then you run the risk of becoming locked into dogma and tradition which is often at the expense of truth, knowledge and understanding. I have designed this course to be challenging but at the same time enjoyable. It will stretch your imagination, skills and abilities and through this process you will discover new levels of self-discipline, control, and personal power. If you haven't already done so, you will begin to take responsibility for your life, your actions and your own ''shit''. Enjoy the course; keep an open mind and an open heart, and above all else a sense of humour. Let go of all self-limitation and accept all that the universe wishes you to receive, if you can your journey, and life will be a lot more interesting and enjoyable.

Reiki Master Teacher Course
One version of the Reiki story.

Although the founder of modern day Reiki, Dr. Usui spent a number of years practicing and teaching ''his system of personal and spiritual development'' later to be called Reiki, he only ever initiated one person into Mastership, his successor Dr. Hayashi. He in turn initiated between 13 & 16 Masters, many of these unfortunately died in the Second World War. One of the people

Dr. Hayashi did initiate, later went on to become his successor and Grand Master, her name was Hawayo Takata, and she had the honour of being the first Non-Japanese Master and the first woman apart from Dr. Hayashi's wife to receive Masters training.

In her time, as Grand Master, Mrs. Takata was instrumental in spreading Reiki throughout the world, and in the process trained a further twenty two Masters, one of which was her grand-daughter Phyllis Furomoto who has taken the title of Grand Master and head of the Reiki Ryoho System Reiki Foundation. From Dr.Usui to Mrs. Takata, the number of Reiki Masters initiated, increased as Reiki developed. Dr. Usui spent his life rediscovering this healing art and then helping others through the knowledge he had learnt. Dr. Hayashi formalised Dr. Usui's teachings giving us the documented hand positions and Reiki symbols. Mrs. Takata played her part by spreading a ''westernised'' accumulated knowledge and experience to the rest of the world.

For some time after Mrs. Takata's death in 1980, there was some confusion as to who could initiate students to the Reiki Master level. Initially it was thought that only a Grand Master could initiate Masters, however when they discovered they could do it themselves, many more Masters began to be trained. Masters brought with them new skills and abilities into their Reiki teaching, adding knowledge, wisdom and healing skills gained through study, life experience and inner guidance. This culture of openness and development does not appear to be reflected in the traditional Reiki Ryoho System, where it is very difficult to be accepted to train as a Reiki practitioner, and harder to become a Reiki Master.

Rigid and formalised, this system requires the student to be vetted and screened throughout their Reiki development with several years training between their Reiki 1 and Reiki 2 attunements. Even after years of training and dedication on the part of the student, they may never pass beyond Reiki 2; they must be invited to do so with very few students being accepted. Those few, who are accepted, must pay fees of between ten and fifteen thousand dollars (in the U.S.A. or Canada, or the equivalent amount in their relevant currency,) during which time they must complete a year's apprenticeship. Once the trainee Master begins to teach, they must do so in the presence of their Mentor/Trainer for a further period of time during which the Mentor/Trainer retains all fees.

Modern/contemporary Reiki has become more accessible to anyone wishing to learn more about it, with the lowering of training fees reflecting this accessibility. Artificial barriers are being swept aside and replaced with an openness and willingness to share knowledge and experiences. This openness needs to be tempered with the need to maintain standards to ensure the principles and precepts of Reiki are paramount, and reflected in the attitude and actions of Master and student alike.

Reiki Master Teacher
Thirty-week course Syllabus

Wk1. Introduction to the aims and objectives of the course

Admin and registration

Student's experiences from levels: 1, 2, 3.

Building their Master portfolio – Seven major sections

Discuss student support/additional requirements

Empowerments - what are they at Master Teacher level

Handout- Manifestation the dream and the reality

Homework- Research stress steroid Cortisol/ DHEA

Wk2. Student's experiences Q&A

Master portfolio-progress Q&A

Discuss the need of establishing a routine – A way to get things done

Discuss effects of Reiki in lives of students and any major changes

Usui's Reiju empowerments, how Usui worked

Begin to develop your own empowerment technique discuss with group

Meditation student led

Reiju empowerment

Handout- Yard Sale (read and discuss next week)

Homework- Produce own Reiki Principles

Wk3. Student's experiences Q&A

Recap last session, discuss homework

Discuss handout - Yard Sale

What exactly is a Reiki Master Teacher: what is their role

Discuss the student's assisting with Reiki courses.

Meditation student led

Reiju empowerments

Homework- Produce 5 I am and 5 I want to be's, share with group

Wk4. Student experiences Q&A

Recap last session, discuss homework

Master Portfolio: progress with handouts in different sections

Use of colour for healing: light/crystals

Meditation student led

Reiju empowerments

Handout- Hatsu Rei Ho technique (information only)

Homework- Research any form of colour therapy/healing

Wk5. Student's experiences Q&A

Recap last session, discuss homework

Crystals: discuss own favourite crystal, and why

Selecting our own healing colour and why

Meditation student led

Reiju empowerments student led

Handout-Darkness, light, colour sound and matter

Homework- Research and discuss in group what a soul mate is

Wk6. Student's experiences Q&A

Recap last session, discuss homework

Master portfolio - progress/problems

Discussing intuition and intuitive techniques.

Reiju empowerments student led

Handout – Intuition (information only).

Handout – Reiji Ho and Byosen

Homework- Intuitive guidance and its use in your Reiki practice.

Wk7. Student's experiences Q&A

Recap last session, discuss homework

Discuss handout – Reiji Ho and Byosen

Discuss the effects, purpose and types of meditation

Meditation student led

Reiju empowerments student led

Homework- Draw your own energy symbol

Wk8. Student's experiences Q&A

Recap last session, discuss homework

Discuss different types of healing energy/cultures

Reiju empowerments student led

Handout- Reiki in Japan today

Homework- Research different cultures/ healing beliefs/practices

Wk9. Student's experiences Q&A

Recap last session, discuss homework

Working with the Mahatma energy

Meditation student led

Reiju empowerments for students in other groups, student led

Handout – Mahatma energy/ meditation

Homework- What do we do out of love and fear

Wk10. Student's experiences Q&A

Recap last session, discuss homework

Discuss the power of the spoken word

Reiju empowerments for students in other groups, student led

Handout- What is the meaning of life

Homework- What are your views on reincarnation

Ensure you have handouts from previous weeks.

Wk11. Student's experiences Q&A

Recap last session, discuss homework

Science and spiritual teachings - how they support one another

Quantum entanglement - how we are all connected

New ways of conveying energy.

Reiju empowerments student led

Homework- Research how science supports spirituality

Homework- Prepare 5 min topic for next week (half of group)

Wk12. Student's experiences Q&A

Recap last session, discuss homework

Discuss development of Master portfolio

Discuss intuitive guidance, psychic ability and Mediumship

Student led talk on topic of own choice.

Reiju empowerments for other groups student led

Homework- Research ''Ascended Masters''

Homework- Prepare 5 min topic for next week (other half of group)

Wk13. Student's experiences Q&A

Recap last session, discuss homework

Miscellaneous energy techniques.

Student led talk topic of own choice

Discuss the common denominator of all healing disciplines

Empowerments student led

Homework- Get information on discipline you know nothing about

Wk14. Student's experiences Q&A

Recap last session, discuss homework

Reiki and the law – Codes of conduct, group to provide examples.

Discuss power of intent, the power of the mind

Empowerments student led

Handout- Energy of the masters, discuss next week

Homework- Define yourself as a Reiki Master, the qualities you bring to Reiki

Wk15. Student's experiences Q&A

Recap last session, discuss handout from last week

Discuss you as a Reiki Master and the qualities you bring

The Chakra wheel – working with intuition and intention

Empowerments student led

Homework- discuss the power of your intent in your daily life

Wk16. Student's experiences Q&A

Recap last session, discuss homework

Preparation for research: student's talk on topic of own choice next week

Empowerments student led

Handout- Holistic approach to personal development

Homework- Explain the difference between tradition and contemporary Reiki

Wk17. Student's experiences Q&A

Recap last session, discuss homework

5-minute talk on subject of own choice

Japanese Reiki techniques

Comparisons with western Reiki techniques

Empowerments student led

Homework- Your views on Eastern and Western style Reiki

Wk18. Student's experiences Q&A

Recap last session, discuss homework

5-minute talk on subject of own choice

Discuss comparisons between Dr Hayashi's and Dr Usui's Reiki manuals

Empowerments student led

Homework- Is Reiki only for those who can afford to pay for it?

Wk19. Student's experiences Q&A

Recap last session, discuss homework

Review students 5 minute talks, how you felt and support received

Review own personal aims and objectives in life

Empowerments student led

Handout- Numerology and life purpose

Homework- Are healers special, if so why, if not why not.

Wk20. Student's experiences Q&A

Recap last session, discuss homework

Traditional Reiki Master empowerments; diagram and instruction

Introduction to Master symbols

Empowerments student led

Handout- Where does God come in

Homework- Study empowerment chart to discuss next week

Ensure you have handouts for previous weeks

Wk21. Student's experiences Q&A

Recap on last session, discuss homework

Discuss Reiki master symbols and their use

Practice traditional empowerments

What makes a good teacher trainer?

Empowerments student led

Handout- Teaching aids

Homework- Produce a simple teaching aid

Wk22. Student's experiences Q&A

Recap on last session, discuss handout and homework

Practice traditional empowerments

Empowerment student led

Handout- Reiki a different perspective

Homework- Revisit your I am, I want to be

Wk23. Student's experiences Q&A

Recap on last session, discuss homework

How we communicate - the words and the silences

Personal barriers to change and development/coping strategies

Empowerments student led

Handouts- Fear Managing change

Homework- discuss freewill and personal responsibility in health and illness

Wk24. Student's experiences Q&A

Recap on last session, discuss homework

Review previous weeks in relation to personal progress

Reiki guides, Spirit guides teachers and guardian angels

Empowerments student led

Handouts- Spirit guides/ The Supernatural and metaphysical

Homework - Why do we forget when we reincarnate?

Wk25. Student's experiences Q&A

Recap on last session, discuss homework

Reiki and the law, codes of conduct, insurance, etc.

Putting the theory into practice in real life terms

Empowerments student led

Handout- The Usui Memorial

Homework- reflect on the content of Usui's Memorial.

Wk26. Student's experiences Q&A

Recap on last session, discuss homework

Discuss different ideas of what success is

Being authentic as opposed to being ''spiritual''

Empowerments student led

Handout- Managing success

Homework- produce your own success list (minimum 15 things)

Wk27. Student's experiences Q&A

Recap on last session, discuss homework

Understanding traumatic stress/stress awareness/coping mechanisms

Meditation techniques.

Empowerments student led

Handout- Stress in the work place/bullying

Homework- produce a simple meditation, 5 min max.

Wk28. Student's experiences Q&A

Recap on last session, discuss students' meditation techniques

Review previous weeks, identify major factors in personal development

Discuss contemporary and traditional teaching methods

Master Portfolio - is it up to date?

Empowerments student led

Handout- The power of words (info only)

Homework- subjects or topics you want to revisit and discuss further

Bring in your master Portfolio's next week

Wk29. Student's experiences Q&A

Recap on last session, topics that need to be revisited

Discuss and review Master Portfolio's

Discuss and put in place additional student support for when course has ended

Discuss if further training is required

Empowerments student led

Homework – think about and discuss with group how far you have come, and the progress made

Wk30. Masters experiences Q&A

Final review and recap of the course

Sharing of Master Teacher personal experiences

Masters portfolios, finishing touches.

Celebration of achievement.

Presentation of Masters Certificates.

Dear friends and fellow Reiki Masters,

If you have reached this point you have come to the end of this particular course but your personal journey continues. As you take your place in the world as a Reiki Master Teacher accept my thanks for allowing me to walk with you for a short while on your journey of discovery, and my gratitude for all that you have taught me.

Chapter 18 - The practicalities of teaching

Professionalism is a word that is often used, and more often misunderstood. If professionalism isn't tempered by compassion it can become cold and uncaring which is in direct opposition to the Reiki principles and precepts. It's important that grounded reality plays a big part in our teaching practice.

We have to accept that some students may never put into practice the skills they have learnt, while others will only use Reiki on themselves, friends and relatives. Some students may however, go on to be Reiki practitioners and it is our duty as their teacher to ensure we provide each and every one of them with the same level of care, attention and support regardless of their ability or aspirations. This is why course notes at Reiki I & 2 and our teaching practice should include advice and guidance on good communication, developing relationships and working in partnership with others, including health professionals. If a student is eventually given the opportunity to work with health workers, they can do so in a way that brings credit not only to themselves but to the Reiki profession.

One of the best ways to teach anything is to demonstrate it and this certainly applies to a professional approach to our students. Our actions, attitude, and manner should all reflect the values we are trying to instil in our students. In becoming a teacher, we also take on the responsibility of becoming a role model and should act accordingly. Part of that role is being true to oneself whilst providing the student with all of the information, knowledge and understanding available that will allow them to take responsibility for their own learning and ultimately be true to themselves. Becoming a Reiki Master faces us with a "paradox" for its only when you have become a Reiki Master, can you begin to understand the level of commitment, knowledge and understanding necessary to achieve that goal.

The level 1 student who makes this decision early on in their training does so in complete ignorance of what is required, like a child who wishes to be an engine driver when they grow up, fascinated by the idea oblivious to the reality. The journey of the Reiki Master is similar in some ways to the novice martial artists as they begin their training; they see the attainment of the *"Black Belt"* as their goal. On achieving this they believe they have reached their destination, and become an 'expert' in their discipline.

The journey for the Reiki Master and martial artist alike brings with it a realisation that at the moment of attainment, the 'Master must become the student again, for the destination sought after is not an end but a beginning for further learning, which is a continual process. The Master and student are both a work in progress; the wise student acknowledges it, the Master truly understands this. Wanting to become a Reiki Master is not a decision that should be taken lightly, for it requires commitment, an attitude of unconditional (non judgmental) love for yourself and for others, the healing of oneself, and most importantly, the empowerment of others through the sharing of knowledge and understanding. A Reiki Master should try to reflect the principles and precepts of Reiki in everything they do, and be an authentic example of the loving power of Reiki. As a teaching Reiki Master you must treat your students with the utmost respect, acknowledging that each one contains a "spiritual spark" that manifests itself as Reiki.

A Reiki Master should try to reflect the **principles** and **precepts** of Reiki in everything they do, and be an authentic example of the **loving power of Reiki**.

It is the responsibility of the Master to connect that "spark" with the student's consciousness enabling them to take control of their own development and destiny, as the Master empowers others, so they become empowered, for what you create for others must come back to you. The Reiki Master constantly works with the energy that fills their life, and in doing so allows it to heal those things that are out of balance or inharmonious. This will lead to the point where this energy, your soul purpose and core essence are aligned and become one. **We no longer do Reiki; we become Reiki.**

Chapter 19 - The duty of any teacher

The duty of a teacher is to educate. We do this, not by telling the student what to think, but by challenging what they already hold to be true. Our role is to guide and help them break free of ignorance and fear formed by conditioning, tradition, and dogma. We dare them to consider new thoughts and ideas that have the power to change their perception of reality and in doing so they can begin to take responsibility for their own learning. It is said that 'we teach what we wish to learn' and in many ways, this is true, for knowledge and understanding never comes to us complete, and on our journey of exploration to find the truth, knowledge and understanding helps illuminate the path that opens up before us as the teacher and student walk side by side.

A Master never seeks to condition or control; they seek to empower by helping the student to free their spirit, and their mind. Their questions should never be seen as a challenge to authority but as an expression of their desire to learn and understand. The dark ages of mankind were unable to hold captive those who had the courage to question what was then held to be true, and overcome the barriers to development, real or imaginary. Education is a physician of the mind and the body, for without the attendance of knowledge and understanding the healing of the patient is impossible. Symptoms of ignorance and fear may be addressed on a superficial level, but the root cause will go untouched.

A closed mind is unaware of its own ignorance and the self-imposed limitations that restrict its development and growth, changed against its will, it remains connect to its roots and will at the first opportunity seek to return to the comfort of the beliefs and values it holds to be true. Education is the only viable means of introducing and maintaining sustainable change in the individual and in society as a whole. Empower a person to take responsibility, think for themselves, and you help free them from the control of conditioning, tradition, and dogma and the many prejudices they help perpetuate. Every student has a personal best and it's the role of the Master to help them achieve it whatever it may be. Everyone has the capacity to learn but some may not be ready and willing to do so. As teachers, we help those that we can, and gently sow the seeds of learning that one day may come to fruition in another time, another place and with teacher who is better suited to the needs of the developing student and ultimately generations to come.

Chapter 20 - Misconceptions of the attunement - empowerment process

Science has a habit of supporting spiritual teachings even though they may first appear to be at odds with one another. For years, science and spiritual teachings were thought by many to be antagonistic yet as ignorance and fear have given way to knowledge and understanding that apparent gap has closed. We have come to realise that both science and spiritual teachings are discussing the same realities albeit in languages alien to one another. That is until quantum physics became the universal language that both the scientist and the teacher could relate to and identify with in relation to their own particular school of thought. Spiritual teachings that were once considered no more than woolly abstract concepts are now being validated by the sciences that provide both the mathematical equations and the necessary evidence to be considered as scientific proof of spiritual truths. Teachers tell us that we are *'beings of light'* and quantum physics now confirm that that all matter, including the human body, consists of waves and particles of light.

Physicists such as Max Planck, David Bohm, and J. S. Bell were able to prove that matter, which includes the physical body, doesn't exist in the way we think it does, and the concept of an 'empty space' is an illusion. When we consider the fabric of the universe, separation is nothing more than a misconception; everything is inexorably connected to everything else, we do not exist **'in'** a universe; we are created as an intrinsic part of a universe that illuminates and animates all things. This has far reaching implications to Reiki students and teachers alike, as we must consider that given such evidence, Reiki, which by our own definition is a universal energy, can't exist separate from the rest of the universe. Reiki is part of creation, as are we, and as such common sense and logic must lead us to the conclusion that we are already connected to Reiki even if we are unaware of the fact.

If this is so, and quantum physics and spiritual teachings appear to support one another in this conclusion, you can't connect through an attunement or empowerment what is already connected. So what purpose does it serve?

Before I offer an answer let us take a moment to consider that there is in excess of 300 Reiki derivatives worldwide, and it's reasonable to accept that all of them will have variations on the teaching and attunement process as part of their training. With all of these variations there has to be a common denominator that links them all together, and there is. If we also accept for a moment they are all 'Reiki' regardless of their brand name or individual identity, then the common denominator has to be 'attention and intention' which allows us to work with the energetic connection that already exists to bring about a desired outcome in the form of raised awareness in the student. Not to connect what is already connected, but to educate the student to the fact that being 'one with the universe' is an established reality and not just a vague spiritual concept.

If we further accept that attunements or empowerments appear to work with all of their variations, we must also accept that structure of the process isn't as important as the attention and intention which underpins the whole procedure no matter what form it takes. A fact that is often overlooked is that no one attuned or empowered Dr Usui. Strip away the details, the story associated with the event and we are left with a moment in time when he became aware, became enlightened to his oneness with the universe. It's recorded that Usui would at times empower/attune his students when he was nowhere near them simply by using his attention and intention. We can disempower ourselves by saying this was Dr Usui and he was able to do things we can't do because of who he was. Or we can adopt a more pragmatic approach and simply accept that he was able to do what he did because he understood, accepted and worked with the realities discussed at the beginning of this chapter. Not as we may have first thought to connect his students to the energy that we call Reiki, but to simply make his students aware of their birthright, and then strengthen the connection that already existed. This he did by raising their level of awareness through increased knowledge and understanding, the basis of all healing, education and awareness. As Usui himself said the only person we can heal is ourselves and we do this by taking ownership for the life we lead and investing time and energy in our health and well-being.

This we can only do when there is a shift in our level of awareness to such an extent that we loosen our grip on perceived reality, and are able to consider new ideas and apply this new found knowledge and understanding in the way we live life.

If you believe we are spiritual beings developing through a physical expression of life, then you must also accept that this connection is infinite regardless of how many transformations it may go through. If however, you believe we are mortal with an indeterminate time between our first and last breath then our physical connection to the universe begins at the moment of our conception and is reinforced at birth. Either way the connection exists; what is missing is the awareness. *So what purpose does the attunement serve?* The attunement is guided learning and a teaching aid; we all learn in different ways and to do this we need to be able to absorb information in a way that resonates with us and makes sense.

Attunements or empowerments work on several levels and provide a physical experience that gives the student a point of reference; a date in their diary to refer back to and say that's when I was connected to the universe. The only thing it can't do is initiate a connection that already exists. If we can accept this train of thought, then it must lead us to a natural conclusion that whatever educates the student to the connection they already have with the universe can be defined as an attunement or empowerment. If on reading this you feel it is a step too far, I would ask you to consider that Dr Usui wasn't attuned or empowered by anyone. His moment of enlightenment came not in the form of an attunement but through the dawning of his own spiritual awareness. Sitting in meditation he realised it was through the existing connection that his journey of spiritual development had gained a new direction, purpose and meaning. It was not to connect but to understand the nature of our relationship to a universe that sustains us. This does not in any way disempower the Reiki Master teacher, if anything it places a greater responsibility on their shoulders to provide ongoing support, to educate and empower their students to gain a greater knowledge and understanding of their relationship with universe and the role we have chosen to play.

Healing in relation to Reiki is a by-product and was never meant to be the defining principle of what Reiki is all about. Reiki is and always has been a discipline of personal spiritual development. It's through this that we educate and then heal ourselves. The only person we can heal is ourselves and we have neither the responsibility nor the authority to arbitrarily heal others. Educate and empower yes; so that they can take ownership and live their lives in such a way that promotes their own health and well-being. As a teacher, you have a duty of care to educate and to challenge students to think for themselves, to ask questions and seek out the truth wherever that may be. To do so is not to dishonour or disrespect what has gone before but to use the established as a solid foundation from which we can gain a new perspective and raise our level of awareness which is the basis of all personal development.

The word Reiki is a label; the problem with labels is that once attached they take on a life of their own and we can then begin to identify more with the packaging instead of the content, and buy into the belief that tradition, manuals, hand positions, symbols and attunements are Reiki. They are not; they are a man made physical interpretations of a spiritual truth. Reiki when stripped back is a distillation of knowledge and understanding, a prerequisite for all education and healing, for without knowledge and understanding neither one would be possible. Attunements have their place in Reiki; they along with the rest of the students training provide a point of reference to which the student can relate to and identify as the start of their Reiki journey. As teachers, we need to be able to put this timeline into context. Their Reiki journey may just be beginning but it comes not as a starting point in life but simply as a continuation of a spiritual journey that began long ago when we became a part of creation. Are we immortal spirit or mere mortal? That is for each of us to decide, for knowledge and understanding never comes to us complete.

No matter when we believe our journey began or where we think our chosen path may lead us, our destination is that of spiritual enlightenment. It is our home, and like the prodigal son of old, it is a place that we will all return to one day.

Chapter 21 - The Master looks to change the cause not the effect

In every situation that you have found yourself in, there has been one common denominator, *you*. You are the one constant in all of the changes you have experienced. All we ever deal with is our stuff and we are the sole creator, the writer and narrator of our own story. We stand at the centre of our universe surrounded by the consequences of our thoughts, beliefs, and actions, we are the cause and they are the effect.

Everything in your life is a reflection, or a projection of yourself; everything in your life is a statement of your intent, past, present, or future. You are the cause and they are the effect, if you want to make lasting changes in your life you must start with the cause, not with the effect, failure to do this will result in momentary improvement until the next batch of *stuff* comes off the production line. It's no good trying to change the effects in our lives; if we keep doing the same things and repeating the same patterns over and over again we will keep getting the same results. The Master knows lasting change comes about when we change the design, this way we control the quality of the product, the effects before they are made. Changing the effects without dealing with the cause is like trying to alter your reflection in a mirror instead of yourself. Lasting change comes about when you look to the cause and then watch the mirror reflect the changes you have made in your thoughts, beliefs, and actions.

If they are fortunate enough every teacher will come to a point in their own development where they question themselves and the validity of their own teaching practices. This point comes when their life and teaching experience begin to challenge tradition and the accepted way of doing things. The teacher is then faced with the decision; do they conform to tradition or do they have the courage to be true to themselves and what they believe in. As teachers, our role is to educate not indoctrinate, we are not here to tell students what to think but to help open their minds so they can begin to think for themselves.

What is hasn't always been so; we often assume that what we do now is the way things have always been done and this applies more so to the way in which Reiki is taught and students are 'attuned' to the energy we have come to know as Reiki. Teachers can only teach what they themselves have learnt, in the way their culture and custom dictates. Usui had no option but to start teaching in the way his traditions dictated but his life experiences helped change the way in which he used that energy to help people, the way he taught his students, and the way in which he opened their minds to the connection that already existed with the life energy that would eventually become known as Reiki.

In a time before Reiki was ever called Reiki it was taught not as a healing discipline but as a life choice that led to a process of spiritual development that brought about self-healing of the student through the acquisition and application of knowledge and understanding. Knowledge and understanding is the vital pre-requisite for any kind of healing be it mind, body or spirit. He quickly realised that the student and patient alike must take personal responsibility for their own health and well-being for without it, the causes of illness and disease remain untouched and compounded due to the person's habitual unhealthy life choices. Symptoms which may appear to be eradicated as healing appears to take place have no option but to return time and time again as the underlying cause goes unrecognised and untouched. Usui's moment of enlightenment or awakening (Satori) came when he realised and accepted his connection to the energy of the universe externally and internally. He understood that as part of creation he could never be separated from its creator or the energy expressed in the form of life and unconditional love.

In the truest sense of the word an attunement or empowerment can be anything that helps the student become aware of the connection they already have with this universal life energy. Dr Usui used a combination of education, instruction, and the power of his own intention to help raise the student's level of awareness to the point where they could grasp the concept of their innate connection to the source and start working with it to make the changes necessary in their lives to bring about healing within themselves. The attunement procedures we recognise today were introduced at a later date as a means of creating structure and formalising the process in a way that made sense Dr Usui's successors and represented their own beliefs and values.

Today Reiki has become a product, a commodity that is in many ways influenced by market forces. As teachers, we are offering a life changing educational package at a price dictated by tradition, market forces or what we believe our time and experience are worth. We do so for philanthropic reasons or to make a living, but either way we are providing a service that will hopefully fulfil their highest expectation and lead to satisfied customers. In days gone by the teacher/student relationship lasted a lifetime that evolved and matured over time, but now we live in a society that demands instant results and often our Reiki training has come to reflect that mindset. Weekend courses costing the student hundreds of pounds are readily available, with one day Reiki master courses for an eye watering £5,000 for anyone who believes there is a shortcut to enlightenment and money is the key to finding it. In many ways, the attunement or empowerment process has come to signify a form of graduation that releases the student from the teachers care, allowing both to move on, the student to build up their own experience, and the teacher to focus on their next intake of students.

As a teacher, I have in the past used the traditional attunement method, but this was when I believed it was only way of connecting the student to the energy source that we call Reiki. Research, life experience and many years of teaching practice have helped me realise that we can't connect what is already connected, we are born connected and our role as teachers is to make the student aware of their relationship with this universal life force.

This we do through knowledge and understanding and an expression of our attention and intention which underwrites and underpins the use of any symbol or procedure we choose to use. Traditional form of attunements work by the nature of this process, as does holding the students hand and having the intention that they become aware of the connection that already exists, which I have done countless times.

Whatever you choose to do is ok as long as it's right for you and you are being true to yourself and you fully understand what you are doing, and more importantly why you are doing it. While you are not connecting them to Reiki, what you are doing is giving them a point of reference, a baseline from which they can measure their own progress and development. There will come a point where they develop sufficiently to recognise and accept their rightful place in the Reiki lineage, both physical and spiritual, their earthly teachers and their own spiritual identity.

Chapter 22 - The kid who could never fit in became a Master who learnt he didn't need to

People wrongly assume that being on your own means you will be lonely, but this isn't always the case. Loneliness isn't a location; it's a state of mind and can be found hidden in plain view amongst the largest of crowds. Victims of loneliness aren't born that way; they are created often as a result of circumstances or other people's actions. Some experts believe that by the age of three we have a clear sense of identity of who we are, and how we fit in with those around us. If this is true our sense of self, our growing knowledge and understanding is more traditional than educational, and this conditioning influences our development from a very early age. Sometimes the conditioning is so well established, so complete, people have no idea of who they really are or what they are capable of achieving. Unfortunately, some go through their whole lives without being aware of this stranger that lives their life. A traumatic event or a life changing wakeup call can pull us up short and get us to stop and re-evaluate our lives, to take a long hard look at what's important, and ask ourselves what we believe in, and think long and hard about the way we are living our life.

The ''pursuit'' of happiness is a futile exercise as we chase after the next emotional fix to raise our spirits. Happiness is an inside job but it's the last place most people think to look to find it. Happiness can be taken from us by another only if we look to them to provide it for us in the first place. We come into this world unbiased, uncluttered, and free from any preconceived ideas about ourselves or those around us. The vast majority of our beliefs, values, fears, and ideas are given to us by others, and we accepted them as our own simply because we knew no different. Those around us automatically become our teachers regardless of whether they are qualified or suitable for the task. During our formative years everyone we come in contact is influential in our lives, the closer the relationship the stronger the bond and the greater the influence and control they exert over us.

The problem we have is teachers can only teach us what they themselves have learnt, and although we eventually begin to create our own experiences, the template for those experiences has already become well established and influences what we believe, and the way we have been conditioned to think. It's only when we take time to re-evaluate those beliefs and values can we begin to gain a baseline of awareness and a growing understanding of *who we are.* It's about discovering the truth about who contributed to making us the way we are. Its only when we begin to understand ourselves can we make conscious decisions as to which of our beliefs and values we wish to retain, develop and call our own. Once we reach this point we must be ready to release and let go of any misplaced guilt we are holding on to. Where once we may have blamed ourselves for every mistake and error of judgement we have ever made, we must now be willing to recognise and accept that those who created us the way we are must take some of the responsibility. Failure to do so means we burden ourselves with guilt while offering the ''model makers'' a free pardon and absolution from the consequences of their actions.

The desire to stand out from the crowd often comes with age and maturity or when circumstances requires a level of creativity that only comes from the ability to think outside of the box. This is virtually impossible to those who are unaware that the box exits, or the possibilities that lie beyond it. Those who fear to stand out will seek the anonymity of the crowd and find comfort in conformity. Their identity and direction will be influenced if not defined by trends and the path of least resistance; they will go along to get along, simply going with the flow.

Chapter 23 - Hey look! I'm no longer broken

If I believe I am broken then it must follow that I will feel damaged, incomplete needing to be fixed. My whole outlook on life will be influenced by that negative mindset, my self-worth, or the lack of it, the relationship I have with myself and everyone around me will be tainted by the thought and belief that life and circumstances have broken me and rendered me worthless. The value we place upon ourselves will dictate the way we allow others to treat us, if we believe we are worthless we shouldn't be surprised when the actions of others supports that self-appraisal, as they treat us in a cheap and shoddy way. Not content to judge ourselves in this way, we use our own values as a template to judge others. Since they don't conform to our belief system we declare them the wrong size, shape, colour, the wrong faith, race or sexual orientation. In our eyes they are different, damaged and broken beyond repair. But damage like beauty is in the eye of the beholder and the life we live is a mirror that reflects and projects the thoughts and beliefs we hold about ourselves. If we change the way we view something, the thing that we are looking at will begin to change to reflect that new mindset. We may look with the eyes but it's our brain that enables us to see, and our mind that allows us to view and value things differently.

The value we place upon ourselves will dictate the way we allow others to treat us.

Perfection is a cruel task master that relentlessly drives us forward to a point on the horizon that is forever out of reach. Unhappy with whom and what we are we constantly look for the next fix, seminar, teacher or relationship that will magically make us whole again. External solutions to an internal problem and when they fail as they must do, we have provided ourselves with even more evidence to prove *"I was right all along, I am broken and damaged beyond repair"*. We look to others to value and love us only when we are unable to do so for ourselves and in doing so we will always be disappointed for healing is an inside job and no one can do it for us. To heal we begin by shifting our focus; we change the quality of our thoughts, the nature and tone of the language we use. We stop referring to ourselves as damaged, for what we focus on we empower, feed and strengthen. We stop discussing 'the problem' and focus instead on solutions, or outcomes we wish to create, at all times raising our personal vibration, our goals and aspirations ever higher. Never lower. This requires a grounded reality to provide a healthy and balance evaluation of where you are and what you want to achieve.

We look to others to value and love us only when we are unable to do so for ourselves and in doing so we will always be disappointed for **healing is an inside job** and no one can do it for us.

You may carry the mental, emotional and physical scars of a hundred battles, but the fact that you can count them is testament

not to you being broken, but to your strength, courage and ability to overcome the hardships you have faced. If you require professional help then you have a responsibility and duty of care to yourself to ensure you get it. It's your life and you alone can live it and when you begin too, its evidence that a change in perception has begun. Battered and bruised but you are a survivor and as such you are faced with a choice. Do you say ''I am broken because of what has happened to me'', or do you say ''I am a fighter and this is what I have achieved in spite of all that has happened to me''. Broken, or distinctive with a depth of character and resilience, the choice is ours to make and the universe will rush to support us in what we hold to be true about ourselves.

Chapter 24 - A survivor's story

We all have a story to tell. The dialogue and characters may change but the back story often remains the same. We are the author and narrator of our life story and the first one in this chapter is part of mine, and reflects the role Reiki played in saving my life and my sanity, long before I even knew it existed.

"I was born into a poor and dysfunctional family. My parents separated when I was young partly due to mother's violence and mental illness, I had an older half-brother, and a younger half-sister who were the result of mother's long term affair whilst married to my father. My father died when I was young and I was left with my mother who had been diagnosed with manic depression (Bipolar) and a personality disorder. She was abused and neglected by both parents as a child. Her mother was uneducated and father was violent towards men, women and children.

Later in life she would baby sit her young nephew. She got angry, lost control and cut his throat with a bread knife. Many years later he would show me the scar, explaining how my mother cut his throat. Once my younger sister and I were made to stand and watch as my mother took a knife to my brother's throat in order to teach us all a lesson.

We lived in various places including a derelict squat. We were all abused and neglected throughout our childhood and into our adult life and this only stopped when our mother died. I became responsible for mother's care at the age of ten when my older brother left school at sixteen and went out to work. My mother became addicted to prescribed barbiturates and amphetamines. A month's supply was usually taken in a week, resulting in periods of being comatose or climbing the walls in withdrawal. I had the job of buying medication for her from neighbours when she had taken all of her own. During these periods, she would walk the streets at night threatening to kill the neighbours with a hammer and carving knife. Screaming, she dared anyone to come out and fight her.

I was prescribed medication for depression at an early age. These experiences resulted in all three of us being f***ked up in our own way. At 18 I finally snapped and attempted to kill my mother by strangling her, I nearly succeeded, but ''something'' saved us both. I would later try to commit suicide, but again fate intervened. I signed myself into a psychiatric hospital as an informal patient. Here I met some wonderful people; patients who frightened me, inspired me and made me feel ashamed for wallowing in self pity.

Within a week I discharged myself accepting that when you hit rock bottom you either stay there or you start climbing. Eventually I would go on to marry to try and get away from a life I hated, not realising the anger, fear and guilt I carried with would affect everything that I did. As a result I wasn't the husband I should have been, or the father I could have been. I was never able to tell my family about the abuse I had suffered because I never really understood the affect and control it had over me. Never the less we would go on to adopt two of my sister's five children who were all placed in care, I became a foster carer for nearly fifteen years looking after children with challenging behaviour, or children who had been abused themselves.

When you hit rock bottom you either stay there or you start **climbing**.

In 1999 at the age of forty-eight the strain became too much to bear and my life literally fell apart. In the space of a few weeks, I was diagnosed with Crohn's disease, my marriage came to an end, I lost my home, and walked away from a job I had come to hate. What appeared to be the end of one life was in fact the beginning of a new one that would take me in a completely different direction. During counselling sessions, I was advised never to have any form of hypnotherapy as this could trigger suppressed traumatic memories that I may not be able to deal with. I began to write profusely and an interest in the spiritual aspect of martial arts eventually led to Reiki which I studied and began to teach. I began to build a new life for myself, working part time to support myself whilst going to college to gain vocational and academic qualification to support my Reiki teaching. I took every opportunity to develop my teaching skills working with as many special needs groups as possible such as SEN, Autism, ADHD, drug and alcohol dependency, anti-social and challenging behaviour in schools, college and in a female psychiatric unit.

I was also able to demonstrate Reiki in a maximum-security prison where I had the opportunity to work with a cross section of inmates including murderers, rapist and paedophiles. In 2006 I remarried and finally felt safe and secure enough to disclose to my wife that I had been abused as a child. My wife knowing me better than I knew myself said ''Now tell me something I didn't already know''.

A fear once spoken began to lose its power to control and now I am able to talk openly about a part of my life that was once very painful. A childhood, that helped create a damaged child, boy and man, each with their own growing burden of guilt for who and what they had become. Evil people never feel guilty in the same way that good people do; that is a self-inflicted punishment of the kind hearted for the mistakes they have made. Mistakes made not from conscious choice, but by conditioning so intense it has the power to mould, deform, and scar. Guilt is the parting gift of the abuser for they have created the victim and the failure the victim perceives themselves to be, a legacy that has the power to corrupt long after the abuse has ended. Guilt has the ability to create a desire to be punished, and the good person will always punish themselves. A mistake is a lesson; not a life sentence of self-inflicted punishment, nor should it be motivation for a continual repayment of a debt that in reality was never owed.

If we can find it in our hearts to forgive the abuser and the role they played in our mistakes, then we must also find it in our hearts to forgive ourselves for until we do we will remain the victim of circumstances long past, and guilt will continue to inflict pain and suffering that is neither deserved or required.

CSJ: my Reiki journey so far.

''My story starts years ago but I will only do the last ten years. The emotions and feelings from leaving the Army and becoming civilian are always a complex mix of fear and uncertainty, but 10 years ago I completely lost the plot. I had lost everything; I was homeless and penniless, but a good friend took me in and provided help, support and a home with hot meals. Let's just say there were ups and downs, a lot of downs for five years.

Then a friend found me help with therapy, and learning new things about myself got me on the road to recovery, to where I am now. Since I have been studying Reiki a few things have changed within me, I now have direction, on a journey moving forward. With my NLP therapy keeping me safe, I'm able to help others. My Reiki energy is amazing, and everything is moving forward nicely as I gain more understanding of myself and others.

Having the confidence to trust people more is a big thing for me. Reiki has helped me to realise I am a nice person inside and people want to see the nice, chill, calm and understanding me where I can put myself first and be ok with it. I have learned not to try and do everything for everyone else, making myself ill in the process, and I now realise people will respect me more for that. Reiki's power of kindness and compassion, it's knowledge and understanding has shown me what I can achieve using my own energy to support others when they need it, while taking the time to help and heal myself.

Reiki and my NLP therapy complement one other and that's great for me. I have a better understand which helps me and others and I now call it git (very) good Reiki if anyone ask me. My Master teacher speaks to me in a language of learning I understand and I am sure we will work together in years to come''.

Anne's story

''For years I felt that it was one crisis after another each one worse than the last. My daughter and 2 of my 6 six grand children were estranged; my son was in active addiction for something like 24 years. His 3 children were cared for by relatives of his partner. My marriage was slowly falling apart. I decided to leave my husband after 31 years together, a massive step to take but one which I have never regretted. During all this I changed my job in manufacturing to working initially as a support worker with

174

people with learning difficulties, then working with older people in the community. Working with people can be so rewarding I actually loved going to work. My health started to give some concerns, I developed some digestive problems, had a cancer scare, high blood pressure, high cholesterol. My GP prescribed various medication one of which was for IBS (irritable bowel syndrome).

Around this time I met Robert who is now my husband, for the first time in my adult life I had found someone that took care of and supported me, because of him my life started to improve. When someone cares for you and offers support in all areas of your life without being judgemental you can start to look at your life and attitudes from a different perspective.

Reiki came into my life, I didn't realise how awesome this was. I had numerous treatments from an amazing lady who actually started my Reiki journey. For this I will be eternally grateful. Andrea made me aware that the years of worry and stress had an adverse effect on my physical health, that my digestive problems were related to the stress I had gone through. By understanding this I was able to stop taking some medication and cope with any flare ups in a different way. It was then that a friend told me about a Reiki 1 class which was soon to start. Little did I know then that the Reiki class and especially the Reiki master taking the class would change my life. This personal development training would transform me and my life to such an extent, absolutely awesome stuff.

I had years of coping with one problem after another often blaming myself for all the bad things, having all this negativity affected me physically and by using my new knowledge, my Reiki, I have been able to forgive myself, let my past go, (not easy but so important) even grow to like the person I have become. I'm an optimistic person and by having a positive attitude rather than negative thoughts I can see a lovely future for me and Robert. I am calmer, happier, healthier, more relaxed and better able to cope with life's ups and downs. Reiki is a way of life that I can't get enough of, believing in myself, being true to myself; it's calming, peaceful, joyful, energising, powerful, unconditional love''.

Carole's story

''Phillip, I'm reading your book 'Pink is the new Black'. Chapters 6&7 which I have just read and then re-read are so powerful and so beautifully written that I cried. They sum up so well how I have felt about myself, I could believe they were written with me in mind. They offer me such wisdom guidance and hope - just as with the Reiki journey I'm now on I feel they offer me a new pathway and a better way to live. I've spent 58 years mentally beating myself up and it hasn't quite worked - so what on earth could I possibly have to 'lose' in this amazing new way to live?

You once said Reiki is in everyone and it comes into our lives when we need it most and I believe that is true. My 'onion' work with a counsellor revealed the problem wasn't what I thought I was seeking help for, but under the layers from childhood.

When it was all stripped away and laid bare the real work began and the reasons for my awful and repeated life choices became uncovered and clear to see and relate to. Then along came your Reiki class and it's helped me so much to piece back my life and never before have I liked nor looked after myself as kindly as I do now. Such a firm basis to grow from, thank you, for opening my eyes to a better way".

Alexandra's story

I really cannot express my thankfulness; you have changed my life. I feel like I'm in peace while reading your work. Reiki has changed my life in so many ways. Thank you so much teacher for everything.

Dave's story

"My 18 month old daughter managed to get cellulitis on one of her eyelids. After days of different types of antibiotics being put into her body with no real results I was feeling quite helpless and really wanted to do something to try and help. By chance I found a contact for Reiki training and decided I had nothing to lose and went for it with an open mind.

I was quite surprised when I was able to feel people's energy around their body as it was completely unexpected. I gave my daughter Reiki straight away and felt like I was actually helping. Day two and my daughter and I fell asleep. She was laid on my chest on the settee, and when I awoke I was surprised to feel my hands tingling as I held my hands on her upper body. I truly believed I was helping her. I'm not saying I cured her but I felt like I had helped to some degree.

She used to get ear ache as young children do so naturally I would apply Reiki to the sore ear. When she learned to speak, without any knowledge of Reiki my daughter would call this 'sparkly hands' and would take a hold of my hand to place it on her ear even when the ear ache had gone, as she obviously enjoyed it. I still practice today and have found that just remembering to try to live my life by the Reiki rules helps me to be a happier and a better person. For that I am grateful''.

Wayne's story

''For some time, I had been asked if I would be interested in going to the local Reiki class. In all honesty, I made many excuses as I thought it was rubbish, but I knew nothing about it. Eventually I said yes, trying to have an open mind as to what to expect. I was made to feel at home and not left out, and got involved with the discussions and Reiki practice that night. At the end of the class I was asked if I would turn up again, and to my

surprise I said yes but due to work commitments I can only attend every other week.

The time I've been going now I have got involved with everything that I can, receiving Reiki from different levels of Reiki students. I have seen, felt and heard things that I couldn't explain. I thoroughly enjoy myself now and look forward to the next class to be involved or observe the next step. It certainly has shown me to never judge a book by its cover''.

Tree's story

''I always thought I had control in my life; that was until I found Reiki Personal Development and, that is when my whole world opened up to all new, weird and wonderful stuff. Reiki to me was all about healing but what I did not know was that I had to heal myself first. Don't get me wrong I still have a long way to go and everyday life still carries on.

I've learned how to deal with stuff from my past but also having to remember that my past has built up over the years and will take some time to fix. To be able to say NO and have control of my life, and that NO is my friend. Learning to deal with stress that most of us has on a daily basis learning to stay calm and speak up for myself and asking for help instead of trying to do things on my own. To be able to say to people who involved me in their everyday life "you know what, this is your stuff not mine" and learning to walk away. Social life was something that I did not

179

have I got up, went to work, came home and went to bed now I have time to fit in the fun stuff and that means leaving my home making new friends and having fun along the way a whole new direction in life and I love it.

One thing that I have learned about Reiki Personal Development is that it's been about me, finding that hidden stranger and learning all over again. What I can say is that my life has totally changed learning how to deal with stress, situations, the past, negative people and the science behind it all but I won't give too much away. So, if like me you want to change your life, Reiki Personal Development can help you heal. Thank you, Philip!''

Darrin's story

''Before being introduced to Reiki personal development by Phillip, my life was a rollercoaster of experiences and interactions with everyone, from family, friends, work colleagues, to strangers on the street. Like most people who feel lost I have been trying to find something to give meaning to life, what are we here for, where am I meant to be. Most of my memories reflect the happiest moments of my life's journey, but, what haunts my never-ending insomnia are the sad and bad spats in my past that I struggle to come to terms with.

The death of family members within a very short space of time left me traumatised. My Father died of prostate cancer. My

180

brother was murdered, and my mother died a month later of ill health. To cope I turned to binge drinking bucket loads of alcohol, wondering the streets looking for a fight, I was hurting and needed to vent that anger, frustration and mis-placed guilt. I tried to distract myself with hours of mindless television and computer games to avoid dealing with life's issues, and heal the pain I felt inside.

I tried for over ten of years to find a balance and purpose in life. I have a gorgeous intelligent wife and two amazing children but I needed more, I needed to work through the pain and confusion, to find myself and discover who I really am.

I have always been able to sense spirit and energies; it was natural and normal to me, and it was through my desire to learn and understand more that I first met Phillip at the Darlington Spiritual Church. I was told he was a Reiki Master, but knew little about it. Phillip was so connected to spirit and with such a calm demeanour; I wondered what is it that makes him such a well-mannered, centred and grounded person, and we became friends.

Neither one of us felt a true connection to some of those within the spiritual church, and drifted away and followed our own path. Sadly loosing contact with people I wished I'd not lost, but little did I realise that time had other plans and our paths were destined to merge once again. I cannot begin to fathom the ways of

181

the Universe; when energies are meant to be together, paths that once diverged lead back to where they are meant to be.

The universe is the ultimate teacher and it used synchronicity to bring us back together again. One of Phillips students came into the tattoo shop where I work, the connection was made. We met for coffee and it was if the bond had never been broken. In Phillip I have found a friend, a mentor and a soul brother, and more importantly I have found myself.

My journey continues; where once I drifted aimlessly, I now have purpose and direction. The sadness I once wished to distance myself from now feels much lighter, and as I continue to heal myself I know the time will come when I can choose what baggage I need to carry with me on the next part of my journey''.

Chapter 25 - A journey of a thousand miles begins with a single step, and a simple question

It's said that a journey of a thousand miles begins with a single step; if this is true then the journey of personal development begins with a single question. A question we often asked as children until we were told to stop asking so many questions, and we unknowingly accepted conditioning as a legitimate means of learning. That initial question of personal enlightenment was to simply ask *'why'*.

This question isn't a challenge; it's a request for an explanation as to why it is so, and this desire to want answers is part of our learning process. Those around us are doing their best to train, educate and inform us, and we as children are doing the best that we can to process and make sense of what we are being told. So when a child is asking 'why' they are trying to fit the pieces of information together so that they can better understand the mental picture that is being created in their mind. If why is the first question to be asked, then it is only one of a number of companions that make this journey together. In many ways these can be considered the five keys to enlightenment that unlock the door that is marked "ignorance and fear". Coincidently they all begin with the letter 'w' and they are why, what, where, when, and who. On their own their power to bring about change is limited, but when united in a concerted effort they can prove unstoppable once the keys have been turned allowing the first cracks to appear in a closed mind.

It's through these ever-widening cracks that the light is able to filter through and eventually illuminate the darkness within. As we grow out of this questioning stage, often with the encouragement of our parents to *'stop asking so many questions'* the time comes when we are introduced to an education system that traditionally seeks not to stimulate minds, but condition them to accept established facts. Historically schools are not places that readily accept challenges to what they are teaching their students, these were, and still are to some degree production lines where the impressionable raw material is fed in one end, and the conditioned, formulated product comes out the other end. Filter systems are in place to assess individual ability and help them to find and accept their appropriate place in society. A conditioned mind is a predictable mind; a mind that is easier to regulate and control, a mind that accepts what it is told, often without question. An open mind, the mind of a free thinker is radical and even revolutionary, that not only seeks to think outside of the box but to remove the belief in all imposed limitations.

Personal development begins when we no longer accept without question. When we challenge the established wisdom and new beliefs in equal measure, and hold them both up to the scrutiny of logic, reasoning and analytical thinking.

A mind once freed will find it impossible to be pigeonholed or constrained by traditions that impose limitations or restrict access to truth, knowledge and understanding to a perceived elite or chosen few. Personal development begins when we no longer accept without question. When we challenge the established wisdom and new beliefs in equal measure, and hold them both up to the scrutiny of logic, reasoning and analytical thinking. Personal development requires the removal of barriers and boundaries we have learned to impose on ourselves, and those deemed necessary by society.

This requires us to learn, before unlearning what we first accepted as the truth, and then the ability to relearn, to accept the knowledge and understanding that lies as yet undiscovered outside of our fabricated sphere of perception. That place in our mind where the impossible becomes our new reality.

Chapter 26 - What price your self-worth?

Based on the current retail value of the mineral content of your body you are worth just over a hundred pounds sterling. If you were to sell off the various components of your body, the brain, bone marrow, vital organs etc your net worth would be millions. Unfortunately, you wouldn't be around to enjoy the benefits of your hard work. Value is subjective and as any sales person will tell you a product is only worth what someone is willing to pay for it, what is trash to one is treasure to another, and a general rule of thumb is you set the value and only get what you pay for.

Need and availability influence what is available to us and the price we are prepared to pay. The more we need something the more we are willing to pay for it, and when something is readily available the less we value it or appreciate its true worth. In today's market how do we set our self-worth? What price do we place upon ourselves as an individual, how do we value ourselves and what price are we willing to pay to be accepted for who and what we are. If value is subjective then the only one that can determine our self-worth is us, and by the same token, what we are prepared to pay in order to achieve personal happiness.

To be true to you, you must first know yourself; and with that knowledge and understanding comes a true sense of worth and value. Until you become aware of who you are, you remain an unknown quantity to yourself and those around you, and susceptible to the selfish needs and demands of others. Until we learn to value ourselves we shouldn't be surprised when those who aren't prepared to invest in a quality relationship, respond to our *"available and open to offers"* mentality and approach to life. If we place ourselves in life's bargain basement we shouldn't be offended by the value people place upon us or the way in which they treat us once we become a part of their lives. We have set the price then allowed ourselves to be bought and paid for, usually at the cost of our peace of mind, health and well-being. We settle for far less than we deserve then live in hope of a miracle that will change everyone around us into caring, loving and considerate people who are able to see and respond to that needy child within. Yet it's this needy child that says *"I will take what I can get and pay the price, just to feel wanted and loved"*. Our external world is a direct reflection and projection of our inner self. Peace or turmoil, it's all the same, and both will find expression in our relationships and the life we lead.

Our external world is a direct reflection and projection of our inner self. Peace or turmoil it's all the same, and both will find expression in our relationships and the life we lead.

What we are prepared to accept and willing to sacrifice to feel wanted, needed and loved will determine the quality of the relationship we have with ourselves, and with those around us. If we don't prize our presence then no one else will, they are simply following our lead. All relationships are based on compromise; if there is no compromise you have a dictatorship not a relationship. Give and take becomes a currency of change in order that the relationship can develop and grow; gaining a depth that goes beyond the superficial physical attraction that lacks permanence and slowly inevitably changes with time.

Compromise isn't the same as being compliant or subservient or making excuses for another person's behaviour in order for them to like you, or be a part of your life. The way in which we treat others and the way in which we allow them to treat us is a clear and precise indicator to the value we place on our self-worth. If we allow ourselves to be used, abused or taken advantage of in any way, knowingly or unknowingly we are sending out the message that this is what we believe we deserve. What we don't challenge we condone and give permission to exist and continue. People will continue to treat you in a way that you allow until you decide that a change in attitude and behaviour is required. They will either value you enough to make the changes necessary to stay in your life, or they will leave in order to find someone who has lower expectation of life and willing to settle for second best, or worse, anything they can get.

> The way in which we treat others and the way in which we allow them to treat us is a clear and precise indicator to the value we place on our **self-worth**.

Self-worth like value is subjective; you and you alone can decide what you are worth, the value you place on your peace of mind, your health and well-being, and the price others will have to pay to be a part of your life and have you in theirs. Knowing oneself is the beginning of true knowledge and understanding, with this awareness comes perspective and an appreciation of who you are your beliefs, values and the principles you hold to be true. You are comfortable with who you are and what you bring to a relationship and the trust, love and respect you expect and require in return. Selling yourself short never leads to lasting happiness and settling for second best always comes at a price that far exceeds what you are getting in return.

Chapter 27 - What greater demonstration of self-love than to heal yourself

If we have never loved ourselves before then it's fair to say that we may not know how to. In this situation if we don't have the answers then we need to seek advice and guidance in order to begin the process of loving ourselves. Every process no matter how simple or complex needs a starting point, a point of reference that we can refer back to in order to clearly identify our goal and measure our progress. Whatever we do must move us towards our goal based on what our point of reference is. If it doesn't then we need to take corrective action to get us back on track and heading in the right direction. Put simply we do more of what moves us forward, and less of what holds us back and sabotages our progress. A problem we face is that the word love although only four letters long, is so big it's almost a concept that lends itself to all manner of interpretations and personal expressions of what we believe love to be. It can appear so big that we feel overwhelmed and powerless when we consider the challenge before us.

It's like standing at the base of a giant obstacle that we must climb and overcome, and when we ask ourselves how are we going to do this the answer is simply one step at a time. If love of oneself is the obstacle we must climb, then the same principle holds true. If love is too big a word for us to manage then we need to break it down into its constituent parts that when experienced individually or collectively we can say *'this is what love means to me'*.

We may all have a different take on these various components that go to make up what we may define as love. To me when I come across compassion, a caring nature respect dignity, truth and a desire for justice then I know love is present. Consideration, open mindedness and the ability to be non judgemental all reflect love in action, so when faced with the challenge of loving ourselves these values become the step by step approach to achieving our goal. When we can be considerate of our own needs, when we can show our self-compassion, care and attention we have begun to love ourselves. When we can look at our faults and virtues in a non judgemental way and see ourselves as neither perfect nor imperfect, but a work in progress that is a product of the life choices we have made, and conditioning we have endured, love is present and seeking expression in our actions.

If we don't know how to, we simply have to be willing to learn how to love. But thinking alone won't get the results we desire. The thought must be energised so that it becomes a belief that will form the foundation upon which our actions can build the reality we wish to experience. If we are willing to learn how to love, then we must take every opportunity to demonstrate that desire. Old habits die hard and established patterns take time and effort to change so we must be ever vigilant to old mindsets and routines where we have demonstrated a lack of love, care, and attention for our well-being and needs as an individual who is deserving of love and affection.

We may wish to rid ourselves of the baggage of fear; anger and guilt in the mistaken belief we don't deserve to be loved because of these imperfections, faults, and failings. This is ignorance and fear at its worst that serves only to keep us trapped within this vicious negative mindset and belief system. By learning to love ourselves unconditionally free from negative judgements we are able to work from a point of strength and personal power. When we begin to take those first faltering steps to learn how to love the person we are, knowledge and understanding automatically replace ignorance and fear, and the burden of anger, fear and guilt will begin to fall away of their own accord. If love is too big for you to handle, simply try being kind and gentle with yourself and this will inevitably lead to the discovery of all of the other components in your life. When we begin ever so slowly to love our self we begin to heal our mind, body, and spirit and what greater demonstration of self-love is there than the desire to heal ourselves.

Chapter 28 - When seeking approval takes the place of our self-worth

A definition of validation is 'to accept, make valid or give approval to'. One of the worst forms of validation is when we allow ourselves to be used, abused or violated in order to gain acceptance or approval from another. When we lack self-esteem and self-worth a void is created that we look to fill in many ways. Unfortunately, this emptiness can't be appeased by food, drugs, casual relationships, or self-abuse.

While it's impossible to satisfy, it can be healed as we increase our knowledge and understanding of self and discover our true worth. Success and achievement are no longer sought to sedate the feelings of inadequacy but as a legitimate expressions of our true self, free from the demands of others and the fear of never being good enough. Once we begin to value ourselves the only validation or approval we seek is our own as personal fulfilment becomes our goal and we let go of the desire to please others at the cost of our own happiness, health and well-being.

Once we begin to value ourselves the only validation or approval we seek is our own as **personal fulfilment** becomes our goal and we let go of the desire to please others at the cost of our own happiness, health, and wellbeing.

Chapter 29 - Lies can be wonderful things, and sweet to our ears

Lies can be wonderful things when their words are sweet to the ears and we have no desire to hear the truth. Lies make great companions when we seek to deceive or hide behind the actions that would otherwise reflect our true character. The most convincing lie is that which contains the greatest element of truth; it entraps the unwary as they hold onto what they wish to be true. In doing so, they unwittingly become prisoners of ignorance and fear. Truth is uncompromising; its hard edges can appear abrupt and unyielding yet, it is often the grain of truth that irritates us more than the words themselves.

Lies must always be dressed up to hide their true image; lies seek to conceal and confuse while the truth seeks to uncover, enlighten and educate. No matter how uncomfortable the truth is, it is better to be freed from ignorance and fear than held captive by a lie.

No matter how uncomfortable the **truth** is, it is better to be freed from ignorance and fear than held captive by a lie.

Chapter 30 - Mirror, mirror on the wall, please tell me, who am I

Healing ourselves may be a lot easier than we think if only we know where to look for the answers we seek. The hard part is getting to know you first in order that the healing process can begin. Healing of any description be it physical, mental, emotional, or spiritual requires knowledge and understanding in order that it can be facilitated. *"There is always something to know before there is something to do"*.

This knowledge and understanding can come in the form of experience, skills and ability of healthcare professionals who have gained a level of knowledge and expertise that is relevant to your needs. In many ways this external expression of knowledge and understanding is very structured, formulated and in many cases prescriptive with an ''illness'' requiring a set of tried and tested responses in order to stabilise and control the condition. Any form of personal or spiritual development should never be at the expense of common sense and logic, nor should we sacrifice our duty of care and personal responsibility at the altar of blind faith, ignorance and fear.

If we need professional help and guidance then it's our responsibility to ensure that we get it, if introspection is required then the same duty of care and personal responsibility must also apply. Spiritual development is never about segregation in any form. Spiritual development requires knowledge and understanding of both the physical body and soul self, the bringing together in knowledge and understanding of the union between the mind, body and the spirit. Each has its own qualities that when unified creates the whole person who must then live and experience life in the physical world with all of the constraints this implies. It is never about making one part of ourselves subservient or submissive to another, for any challenge for supremacy no matter how spiritual the banner it flies will trigger a response and resistance. Lines are drawn and the battle commences. Unfortunately, this is a battle where we arm both sides, and our body becomes the battleground.

Setting out on this journey of introspection, one of the first steps we must take is to accept that we are initially totally unprepared and unsuitable for this particular quest. Unprepared because we have no real understanding of who we are, and unsuitable, because of our innate ability to lie to others, and more importantly lie to ourselves about the nature of our physical, mental, emotional, and spiritual state of health. The one saving grace we have is that our body never lies. Our body is a mirror of truth that reflects clearly our true state of health, even when ignorance and fear becomes our comfort blanket and we look to shift the blame and responsibility onto others for the state of our health and the life we lead. To heal oneself you must first come to know oneself. True knowledge of self or anything else comes with understanding, which should then equate to remedial action that forms part of the healing process.

When we begin to know better, comes the responsibility to do better, but responsibility can never be given and can only be accepted by those who wish to bring about change in their lives. This requires us to question and re-evaluate our thoughts, beliefs and values and the negative debilitating life choices we may be making on a daily basis. In a world defined by modern technology ignorance becomes a matter of personal choice, and a state of bliss that hides a multitude of sins and unwise choices we make on a daily basis on the pretext of not knowing any better. If ignorance becomes our chosen fix, it becomes almost impossible to awaken the person who pretends to be asleep, and refuses to look into their mirror of truth and ask the question, Mirror, mirror on the wall, tell me who am I.

Mirror, mirror on the wall, tell me who am I.

Chapter 31 - Where there is blame, there's a claim it wasn't your fault

Human nature being what it is, the minute something goes wrong in our life we look for someone to blame. We either blame someone else regardless of whether it's their fault or not, if we suffer from low self-esteem we mistakenly believe that this problem like all others is automatically our fault. Even when caught making a simple mistake or doing something wrong, we will often go to great lengths to justify our actions and defend ourselves. Even to the point of blaming the other person for our actions, it's almost like we had a right to do what we did because of the other person or the situation.

The root cause of all of our conscious actions is a creative belief that formulates our lives and everything in it. We do what we do because it serves a purpose no matter how negative or self-destructive our actions may appear. The police say "to understand a crime you need to understand the motive", for us to understand our own behaviour or anyone else we need to understand the creative belief that determines who we are, and why we do what we do. Mistakes can be seen as a natural part of our personal growth and development, and not indicative of being in any way a bad person. Blame can seem like a natural and justified reaction, but blame for its own sake can lead us into a dead end of resentment and recrimination. Accepting responsibility for our actions is a creative response that can lead to development and growth, but true responsibility only comes with knowledge and understanding. Once we begin to understand why we think and act in a way we do, we can direct our intention towards change rather than repetition, a positive response rather than a negative reaction. Attention and intention is our belief in action; it is the power of positive change, we do only what we believe is possible, and the quality of our intention determines the quality of our actions and attitude we present to others.

Every challenge will trigger a response in some form or another, when we apportion blame we are challenging a belief and indirectly the person that holds that belief. Every action we take brings with it a set of consequences that must then be dealt with in order to move forward. We are motivated, directed, and defined by our self-belief, our relationship to the world we live in and the people around us. Understand the nature of the belief and you will begin to understand the person that holds those beliefs and the life they lead. From this we can see that knowing oneself is the beginning of true knowledge and understanding and the end of the need to blame ourselves, or anyone else.

Knowing oneself is the beginning of true knowledge and understanding and the end of the need to blame ourselves, or anyone else.

Chapter 32 - The future is your child in time; already conceived but not yet born.

It's human nature to want to put as much distance between ourselves and anything we want to release or get rid of. When taking out the garbage that's fine, but when it comes to letting go of rubbish from our past sometimes the opposite approach is required. To release the past, we may have to revisit places from our childhood or formative years, to compare and connect the reality to the memory. When we revisit places that have claimed a place in our memories and emotions and we see how little they have changed over the years, time appears to have stood still. In that moment of reflection comes clarity and perspective, we begin to see how much we ourselves have changed and moved on.

No matter how much we wish to separate ourselves from the past we can't. The past is as much a part of us as the present moment and the future is. The past is the parent to this present moment; the future is the child in time, already conceived but not yet born. If we see the past as an adversary who must be fought in order to gain a foothold on our future, then the battle will be never ending. The greatest foe we face is ourselves, and this internal power struggle has the potential to destroy us if we let it. The past didn't just happen; it was created and as such it has as much right to exist as the present and the future has. It will not and cannot be denied. The pain we sometimes experience is not from the past itself but the conflict that comes from our reluctance to acknowledge that the past was instrumental to the creation of the person we have become. In many ways, the past is the teacher that presents us with the lesson in the here and now. If we are wise enough to learn from it the future becomes the truth demonstrated.

The pain we sometimes experience is not from the past itself but the conflict that comes from our reluctance to acknowledge that the past was instrumental to the creation of the person we have become.

The past once created cannot be undone but it can become worn by the passage of time and the result our many visits. Every time we revisit the past we leave a piece of ourselves there, and bring a fragment of the past into the present moment thus strengthening the very bonds we wish to break. Time presents us with an opportunity to move on, a chance to gain perspective if we would just acknowledge the debt we owe to our past, and make peace in order that the fragmented self can be made whole. It is impossible to heal the self without having the willingness and the desire to love and forgive oneself for past mistakes and perceived imperfections. The guilt we hold on to does not come from love. Guilt is the ego's way of exerting dominance and control, like a vengeful domineering parent that must be obeyed at all times. Freedom and healing comes when we accept that no one out ranks us when it comes to the authority of ourselves, we are the undisputed and powerful CEO of Self Inc.

Freedom and **healing** comes when we accept that no one out ranks us when it comes to the authority of ourselves, we are the undisputed and powerful **CEO** of **Self Inc.**

The greatest weapon that can be used against anyone is the power of their own ignorance, and the negative ego is a past master at using our own ignorance and fear to make us believe we are powerless and deserving of punishment for past mistakes. If no one is available to punish us then in our ignorance we are more than happy to take on that responsibility, in the process inflicting punishment on ourselves that is disproportionate to the perceived 'offence' and is neither deserving nor required.

We are born into an imperfect world with the (soul) purpose to learn, develop and grow. The desire for perfection is at odds with the task at hand which is to make mistakes, to learn from them and in doing so develop physically and spiritually. Success without failure teaches us nothing. We celebrate success giving little thought to the process that brought about the achievement. Failure demands our attention and with it an inquisition as to what went wrong. Lacking knowledge and understanding we can allow negativity to raise its ugly head with the need to blame and hold someone accountable, with an ensuing guilt trip that can last a life time.

Letting go does not require us to feel guilty or obligated to our past mistakes; guilt is a choice that is both destructive and counterproductive and serves no purpose other than self imposed punishment and attachment to a past real or imaginary. Letting go of the past requires us to be honest with ourselves and accept that mistakes were made, and while ignorance covers a multitude of sins it also encompasses a lifetime of experiences that demanded we make choices often without the life experience to do so, or little realising the consequences of our actions. We are not asked or

expected to be perfect. We are simply asked to do the best that we can with what knowledge and understanding we have available to us at the time, and when we know better, to do better.

Mistakes do not denote a bad person; they signify a work in progress whose faults when overcome stand not to devalue and diminish, but to praise the progress made in face of the challenges that had to be overcome. Taking time to return to where it all began can, with the right mindset, be a major part of the healing process. We are not there to dwell on the past but to draw a line under it and in doing so accept that what debt there was has been paid in full by the sacrifice of our peace of mind. We have come to make peace with our past; we may not yet be the best of friends, but we are still able to part on good terms.

Chapter 33 - Enlightenment and the shadows it casts

"The dark side of enlightenment is a place of shadows where ignorance and fear prevail. Like a closed mind it's unaware of its own ignorance and can see no further than the limitations formed by its own debilitating beliefs'. This is a place where Knowledge and understanding appear as strangers travelling in a foreign land".

Healing can't be considered complete until it touches the mind, body, and spirit. To heal is to literally make whole, to bring together and consolidate, and as such healing of the physical body can't be considered in isolation. The most important part of the healing process is for each of us to make the connection between our internal thought processes and beliefs and the external realities they create through the life choices we make. In this way education and healing walk hand in hand. Good health has to be more than just the absence of pain, illness or disease. It must also include knowledge and understanding of what constitutes good health and the part we play in the process.

The most important part of the healing process is for each of us to make the connection between our **internal thought processes and beliefs** and **the external realities** they create through the life choices we make.

An error is not a mistake unless we are unwilling to acknowledge it and then take corrective action, but what's created in error will be repeated unless steps are taken to correct the mindset that was instrumental in creating the problems experienced as illness and disease. Nothing exists in isolation; everything playing its part, each with a clearly defined role and a collective responsibility that makes the whole greater than the total sum of its many individual parts.

To claim ownership for the healing of anyone other than ourselves is misguided and demonstrates a lack of understanding in the healing process, and the nature of the energy we work with. We are not creators of healing; we are facilitators whose 'soul' purpose and primary objective is to heal ourselves. In doing so we gain the necessary experience, knowledge and understanding to enable us to help others heal themselves, free from a victim mentality and a major investor in their own health and well-being. The energy we work with was instrumental in our creation. Infinite by definition it can never be confined or defined by the labels or names we place on it. We can neither add to it nor detract from it in any way by our presence or how we choose to use it. It is the ultimate free gift that can't be earned or paid for and requires nought but our acceptance. Once accepted its use is optional in line with the life choices we make and the exercising of our free will which is sacrosanct.

Put simply we are channels and the prime directive of any channel is to first heal itself. To clear out the debris, the silted-up residue created by years of ignorance and fear, and the habitual unhealthy life choices made on a daily basis. In healing the self, we ensure the channel is as good as it can be and doesn't restrict in any way, so when this healing energy flows it does so unimpeded, and reaches the intended recipient. The greater need will always be addressed first regardless of ownership or the labels it carries, be that of recipient or practitioner. Our attention and intention simply acknowledges the source of the healing and our readiness to work with it in a non-obtrusive way. Since we are not the primary healers the process doesn't require our creative input as there is nothing for us to claim ownership to. There is nothing for us to do other than facilitate the process then get our negative ego and its mental and emotional baggage out of the way.

Through the healing of oneself we are able to recognise and accept our role, we are educators who facilitate knowledge and understanding, our role is to act as an example of the power of the individual to heal incrementally one step at a time. In doing so each person becomes living proof of this truth demonstrated. We do not create or produce this healing energy. We facilitate, we connect and then get out of the way so that the energy flows to where it is needed. Our aim is to reduce our involvement to the point where we appear to do nothing, yet everything is done that needs to be done. Relationships of any description need commitment and a desire to make them work. Physical relationships need investments and spiritual relationships need clarity. The purpose of life is to make that spiritual connection that transcends the physical illusion of what is real and permanent.

Energy is the be all and end all, it's all there is. What we consider real is nothing more that our understanding and interpretation of the energy field that we are a part of. What we perceive as a physical world is only possible through the limitations of our physical senses that provide us with apparent form and structure. Yet as a species ours is only one level of reality. The earth that sustains us and creation we share our planet with are able to see, hear, feel, and sense a world just as real that is far beyond out limited abilities and perceptions. In many ways, our misguided sense of superiority is our greatest failing and barrier to our physical and spiritual development.

If knowledge and understanding are the prerequisites for healing of any description, then they must also be an expression of that creative energy. The words themselves, the sounds they make and the way they appear before us. Frequency is the chosen mode of transport for energy; knowledge and understanding is a frequency as are the states of health and well-being and the purpose of our mind is to tune into the frequencies of health and happiness, illness and disease which manifest themselves at a cellular level. Put simply our psychology becomes our biology. Healing against a person's will or in ignorance of the part they play offers nothing more than a temporary reprieve from their condition. A postponement to the inevitable return of their illness as the symptom is addressed but the underlying cause goes unchallenged and untouched, the root cause left to re-establish itself.

Ignorance in the form of lacking knowledge and understanding can hide a multitude of 'sins' and is unaware of its own closed mind. Not everyone who is ill or unhealthy is able to acknowledge the part they play in the process or let go of the ''negative frequencies'' in the form of thoughts, beliefs, and actions. If we accept cause and effect as a major player, then we also have to accept that good health and illness have a beginning and an end.

Chapter 34 - As one journey ends another begins

Life is a journey that many complete without ever realising its true purpose, its meaning or recognise the opportunities missed along the way to learn and grow. A gift of life that comes without guarantees; an indeterminate time between our first and last breath to navigate our way past the obstacles and pitfalls that litter our chosen path. A path often chosen for us before we are born, but a path none the less that allows us if we so wish, to break new ground and old beliefs in equal measure. To the seeker of knowledge and understanding the path they are on is always the right one, and they trust that the universe is guiding their faltering steps. A life whose value is reflected in our beliefs; beliefs handed down from generation to generation like a family heirloom to be protected at all costs and defended to the death from those who we perceive to be different from us, in colour, creed, or faith.

Differences so ingrained in the closed minds of those unaware of their own ignorance, yet differences that are no more than skin deep to those with the eyes to see the reality before them.

The meaning of life is a paradox; it is both simple and profound as seen in the eye of the beholder. Simplicity in as much as the meaning of life is what you want it to be. Your beliefs and values help determine your purpose in life and its meaning. If you are driven to be wealthy and have an abundance of material possessions, then the achievement of that goal gives meaning to your life. The danger is that the more we have the more we want and we become owned by the things we desire to possess. Then we fear losing those things that have become a status symbol and a testament to who we are in our own mind, and in the eyes of those who can see no further than the trappings of materialistic success. But no path is higher or lower than another, and we must find our own way for it's our life and we alone can live it. Sometimes we must complete the journey before hindsight provides the clarity of vision not available as we struggle from day to day. Lessons not appreciated at the time, which only become relevant when age and the maturity it can bring, help us to change both beliefs and values and appreciate the missed opportunities that life had to offer. In those moments of quiet contemplation, we regret time lost, misplaced and misused, that can never be reclaimed. Silently we ask ourselves ''what if'', and wonder ''what could have been''.

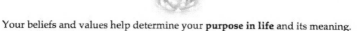

Your beliefs and values help determine your **purpose in life** and its meaning.

Those who believe there is more to life, a hidden meaning waiting to be discovered commit the time and effort to seek out the true holy grail of knowledge and understanding. There is a stranger that lives our life that we must first get to know, befriend accept and understand. If forgiveness is required, it must be given unconditionally for this person will become your travelling companion on your journey of self-discovery. The words you read are nothing more than signposts to help you find your own path. Along the way you may discover the true meaning of your life is defined not by what life can give you, but by what you give to life. To give to those less fortunate who are able to give nothing but their gratitude in return for the kindness you have shown them. The first step is always the hardest and the journey is always easier without unnecessary baggage to weigh us down and slow our progress, but only we can decide what to keep and what is safe to be left behind. Baggage, once so important to us, but now no longer reflects who we were, who we are, or more importantly, the person we chosen to become.

The true meaning of your life is defined not by what life can give you,
but by what you give to life.

Chapter 35 - Me, myself and I, a partnership for change

Whatever we do repeatedly we do so for a reason or a reward. The habits we develop and the experiences we create no matter how negative fulfil a deep-seated need within us. This need is linked directly to a belief we hold about ourselves, if you change the belief you will ultimately change the habit and the corresponding experience it creates. Awareness that comes with knowledge and understanding is the first step in any form of change, be it a direction in life or the healing of oneself. Every situation we experience is in the same moment a combination of the past, present and future rolled into one. Action taken in the past created the present moment, and what we do now will create a future we must experience and live through. To know where you want to be you must first understand where you are and what brought you to this place in time; this provides a point of departure and a destination, a place or a state of mind. Knowing change is required is only the first step; knowing we have a problem is one thing but knowing what to do about it is another. This is where a partnership for change can begin to create a positive effect in our lives.

Teachers and signs have a lot in common; they don't tell you what you must do, their role is to simply point the way and if necessary provide directions. All any teacher can hope to do is bring about that initial state of awareness by helping the student take responsibility for their own learning. A teacher's role is to show the way but never impose limitations by telling the student what they must see, or what they must think. Personal development is just that and each one of us has a responsibility and duty of care to our own health and well-being because no one else can do it for us. The choice always rests with us as to whether we make the changes necessary or we choose to stay the way we are bogged down by old habits and stale routines, or worst still immobilised by ignorance and fears.

We must have the determination to make the necessary changes, knowing where you want to go and knowing how to get there is one thing but planning and preparation in itself won't get the job done or achieve your goal. Sooner or later you have to take the first faltering steps on your journey, a new and exciting adventure or a journey of self-discovery to get to know the person you have become, the principles are exactly the same. At some point, you will have to let go of the past and commit your time and energy to a new course of action in order for you to achieve lasting and sustainable change in your life. Others can provide the knowledge and understanding and help point the way but you must have the desire, belief and determination to make it happen. A belief no matter how deep seated is no more than a feeling of certainty. We are certain of our beliefs and what we are able to achieve, and whatever we believe about ourselves becomes our truth, and it's those beliefs we hold about ourselves that helps form the world and the future we create.

Chapter 36 - Change always creates resistance

Change of any description will always create resistance. Resistance from those around us who don't want us to change for their own selfish reasons, and resistance from ourselves as old habits die hard and won't give up without a fight. If we have the option of change we will always take the path of least resistance, which usually means we stick with what we know best even if it's bad for us. Change is often a last resort or when we no longer have a choice in the matter.

From a personal point of view it sometimes feels like we have to reach the end of our tether, or hit rock bottom before we are motivated to change our lives in some way, we finally reach the point where we can't go on, but at the same time feel powerless to do anything about the situation we find ourselves in. Ignorance and fear keep us locked into a situation awash with negative emotions such as resentment, anger and guilt, all of which are unhealthy and poison to our mind and body. On the way down we may feel like we are in freefall and totally out of control, but rock bottom provides a solid foundation on which to build something better for yourself. You have a choice, do you give up and sit in the dark, or do you start to climb towards the light. Are you worth the effort to create the kind of life you deserve, the decision you make will be decided by the belief you have in yourself and the value you place on your happiness.

You have a choice, do you give up and sit in the dark, or do you start to climb towards the light. Are you worth the effort to create the kind of life you deserve, the decision you make will be decided by the belief you have in yourself and the value you place on your **happiness.**

In many ways change is inevitable, but personal development is a choice we have to make once we realise it's possible, we deserve to be happy and have the right to expect nothing but the best for ourselves, and the best from those who want us in their lives. Compromise is necessary in any relationship but true compromise is a delicate balance of give and take that's fair for both parties and in equal measure. The mistake we make is to undervalue our own self worth and sacrifice our happiness in the belief that we are responsible for the other person's happiness. Loving unconditionally is not the same as loving irresponsibly; loving unconditionally comes from a place of emotional maturity and grounded self-awareness. We act irresponsibly when we continually give to others without getting any response, in the forlorn hope that they will change and begin to love and appreciate us in return. Love that has to be bought or forced is not love, but a desperate need looking to be satisfied, and the abuser neither likes nor loves the person they take advantage of. If they did, they would never do it in the first place.

This kind of personal development is rarely if ever an easy option, and given our determination to hang on at all costs, more often than not circumstances have to intervene, contrive as they do to bring us to a point of separation, an appointment with fate. Here paths cross, and we are introduced to kindred spirits, shared experiences and the courage to let go of what can't be changed. Strangers who become friends, who challenge and inspire us in equal measure to love ourselves just enough to release our grip on those who's hold is not to caress but to control and to keep us trapped in the debilitating belief that change is only possible for those far more deserving.

Chapter 37 - You are going to fail in life, but that's ok

Being positive is a wonderful thing but you must be realistic. Do a bit of personal research and you will find that the great spiritual teachers were positive in their outlook but also grounded in their attitude to life. They advocated positive change but they also recognised the realities of everyday life that made those changes necessary. They may have taught about raising awareness, but their feet were very firmly on the ground for they understood to change any situation you must first accept it for what it is.

Reality can be harsh and unyielding and we can be tempted to retreat into a world of make believe, but illusion lacks real substance and offers cold comfort when having to face the challenges life presents us with. Fearing failure or lacking belief in our own ability we go for the safe option, we do what we really don't want to do in the mistaken belief that we are in some way stacking the odds of success in our favour. Unfortunately, life has a habit of throwing us a curve ball, and the best laid plans have a habit of going "tits up" when we least expect it. If we live in the land of make believe we can ensure life is perfect, but real life is made up of highs and lows, successes and failures which provide purpose, meaning and value to the life we lead. We have to make choices on a daily basis and hopefully those choices are considered and informed, but fear can disempower even the most positive person and trick them into playing it safe. It's inevitable we will fail but surely it's better that we try and fail doing something we feel inspired to do, rather than settle for an easier option that may satisfy our physical needs but starves our spirit, and leads to an unfulfilled life.

It's better that we try and fail doing something we feel inspired to do, rather than settle for an easier option that may satisfy our physical needs but starves our spirit, and leads to an unfulfilled life.

Chapter 38 - A dose of reality is the only cure for an illusion

Personal development is a wonderful thing but being so close to the problem we can't always see the solution that's in front of us. We desire to embrace the healing spirit of nature, but are unable to see the woods for the trees. We look for a solution to a problem unaware or unsure of where it may be found, we desire to let go of unwanted baggage yet are totally unaware of what we are hanging onto or why. We believe our life story is unique to us yet it's a narrative that we all share, the characters may be different and the names may change but the back story, our story, the ability to love oneself unconditionally is truly universal and applies to each and every one of us. Our story may be co-authored by others at a time when we appeared to have little or no say in what happened in our lives, but we must take responsibility for the story we have repeatedly told ourselves until it becomes our unquestioned, unchallenged yet unsound reality. A reality that is no more than an illusion accepted in error as the truth.

Over the last few days this was brought home to me in a very painful yet liberating way. In 1999 I was diagnosed with Chron's disease which is a condition where the body's immune system fights an imaginary infection damaging itself in the process. Once I understood the symptoms I quickly realised I had suffered with this condition for many years prior to being diagnosed with it. Temporary relief came in the form of major surgery that saw the condition alleviated for over sixteen years which was ended by a flare up that coincided with my decision to retire from fulltime employment and concentrate on my writing and teaching Reiki as a true form of self healing and personal development.

The flare up painful as it was, raised an age-old question of what I was hanging onto that was contributing to the condition rearing its ugly head again after so long to cause me so much pain and discomfort. This was a question I had asked so many times without ever discovering the answer, but this time was different for the answer when it came, did so from the most unlikely of sources.

The life story I had written contained a chapter which detailed in my mind at least, the cause and the creator of this horrible condition that was affecting my life. This I attributed to an abusive childhood and a ruptured appendix at an early age which I also accredited to the actions of my abuser. This was the story I had told myself so many times it had become ingrained in my psyche and the stuff of legend. Although the abuse and neglect was both real and terrifying, the back story was nothing more than an illusion, a figment of my imagination. Having just spent three days in hospital receiving treatment I was lucky enough to be examined by a consultant that helped me understand that reality is the only cure for any illusion. That part of my story was based on my own ignorance and fear, but was firmly but compassionately rewritten by the doctor as he explained that Chron's is a medical condition that isn't caused by the actions of another person no matter how cruel and abusive they may be. Nor is it created as I first thought by fear, stress, and anxiety, but as he explained these negative emotions enflame an already painful condition. His final words were to accept and release the condition for what it is instead of holding onto the painful illusion of what I had convinced myself to be true. The final part of the answer came from the most unlikely source, the condition itself.

Once I became aware of this disease it became an enemy that had to be overcome, to be defeated and got rid of at all costs. When I was forced to think about it or its effects on my body it was with the harmful and negative emotions of anger, resentment, and fear. In my version of events these were legitimate weapons to use against an enemy of this kind, but reality forced me to face the fact that my negative emotions were ineffective against the illusion and I was harming no one but myself. Anger, resentment, fear, and anxiety are negative emotions that have the power to destroy life and when these destructive forces are directed at a condition that feeds on this power there can be only one outcome, the continuance of pain and suffering.

We are the author and narrator of our life story, be it real or imaginary and in our efforts to write a new life affirming chapter we may need to first revisit the past to re-evaluate and rewrite some parts that owe more to well meaning fantasy, than fact and reality. In doing so we must be careful not to simply adopt a victim mentality believing we are powerless and there is nothing we can do. Before any situation can be changed it must be first accepted for what it is, the self-imposed illusions must be seen for what they are, and reality as the cure for debilitating misguided beliefs. In any situation in life there is always something to know and understand before there is something to do, and personal development is no different. Stories repeated so many times they become justification for living a life we have created yet want to break free from.

Sometimes the act of letting go is easier than we think, and the answers are where we least expect to find them, but we must first take the time to find out what's real and imaginary. The mirage is often nothing more than a reflection of what we want or expect to see and to the person lost, the reality is hard to see and even harder to accept.

Chapter 39 - How do I love someone I don't know?

When it comes to personal and spiritual development it is often said one of the first steps is to learn to love ourselves. This is a beautiful concept that lends itself to all manner of affirmations and mantras designed to help us reach this point of enlightenment, unfortunately, like many things in life it's far easier said than done. For a start, the principle of loving yourself works on the assumption that you actually know the person you are trying to love. The problem I have with this concept is I don't know who I am, and I have yet to meet anyone who can honestly say they truly know and understand themselves. If we think about it, a commitment to any form personal and spiritual development works on the premise that we are committed to taking a journey of self-discovery during which we hope to gain a better understanding of who we are, and reach a point in time where we gain clarity and insight.

As the old saying goes *''a stranger is just a friend we have yet to know''* and in any relationship, we have to take time to get to know that person, to build up a rapport with them to the point where we feel comfortable and at ease in their company. The stronger and deeper the relationship the more we can relax and simply be ourselves, letting go of the need to pretend or act in a certain way, and hopefully be accepted for who we are. Before I can begin to love myself, I need to understand what love is and then get to know the stranger that lives my life. My first step on this particular leg of my journey is to try and understand the true nature of the love I must begin to show to myself. The term love is often applied in broad sweeping brush strokes, a generalisation that overlooks the elements that make it possible. Respect, dignity, compassion, and consideration not only make love possible, they make it applicable in situations requiring its healing presence.

Before I can begin to love myself, I need to understand what love is and then get to know the stranger that lives my life.

These are the pillars which support the emotions. When we reduce the concept of love to its basic components we discover that love is healing by another name, transcending the emotional feel good factor often mistaken for love itself. Healing takes place when knowledge and understanding are present, and when faced with the challenge of loving oneself the depth of love will be defined by the depth of self-knowledge and understanding required for healing to take place.

*If our aim is to **love ourselves** then we must find it in our heart to apply those principles of respect, dignity, compassion, and consideration to ourselves in the same way we would to any other person we care for.*

To know oneself is the beginning of true knowledge and understanding. If our aim is to love ourselves then we must find it in our heart to apply those principles of respect, dignity, compassion, and consideration to ourselves in the same way we would to any other person we care for. The relationship we have with ourselves is often the most neglected yet it's the level of intimacy we nurture with ourselves that defines the quality of relationships we share with others. We all possess the ability to love our self but some choose to withhold that love because they feel they don't deserve it because of mistakes they have made. In withholding love and the healing it brings they are overlooking a basic fundamental principle of life, and the basis of all personal and spiritual development. Mistakes are an integral part of our personal and spiritual evolution.

Mistakes provide the ideal growing conditions for future development and success. Success is the finished article whereas mistakes reflect the potential of a work in progress. We celebrate success without giving much thought as to the way in which it was achieved, by contrast our mistakes are clinically dissected, and blame is apportioned often without the chance of redemption through good deeds when we come to know better. In the dark recesses of our minds lurks that harsh judgemental parent figure that would have us believe that the making of mistakes makes us a bad person deserving of punishment. In the absence of someone to punish us we take on that role and withholding love becomes an insidious form of self-abuse. Mistakes do not automatically make us a bad person they make us human; we are neither perfect nor imperfect we are simply a work in progress whose 'soul' purpose is to develop and grow. Character and personality form at an early age, only for time to cover them with the dust and debris of life's experiences, we age and change to the point we no longer recognise the reflection in the mirror.

With age comes perspective and hindsight is a wonderful thing; looking back allows us to see how far we have travelled and transitions that may have taken place along the way. In hindsight, I can honestly say I'm no longer the person I used to be, and there are times in moments of quiet reflection I struggle to recognise or be at peace with who I once was. The specter of childhood abuse and neglect cast a long shadow in my life and the burden of anger, guilt and poor self-worth was carried for many years. In the daily battle for my mind there were casualties, collateral damage as I failed those around me, loved ones who were unaware of the stranger that shared their life. Do I love myself? No I can't in all honesty say I do just yet. What I can say is that the more I come to know and understand about myself the more I am able to let go of harsh judgement and negative criticism. Each time I find the courage to confront my own ignorance and fear, be it in the past, present or the future I create space, room in my life for respect, dignity, compassion, and consideration to develop and grow.

I am neither perfect nor imperfect I am simply a work in progress looking to improve on who I was yesterday. The ability to love myself may come in time, but for now I am happy just to get to know the stranger that lives my life and who is patiently waiting to become a very good friend of mine.

I am neither perfect nor imperfect
I am simply **a work in progress** looking to improve on who I was yesterday.

Chapter 40 - Forgiveness! Isn't that just for spiritual people?

The topic of forgiveness often comes up when I discuss personal development with my students, and the need to dispel a few myths and misconceptions associated with forgiveness. Firstly, there is this mistaken belief that being able to forgive makes you a better and more spiritual person than someone who doesn't have the ability to forgive. Not only is this not true, it's ego based bullshit. Being able to forgive means you have learnt a particular skill that has proven benefits, and you have enough sense to stick with it, but in other aspects of your life you could still be a complete self centred prick. Forgiveness is only one small piece in the jigsaw, and you need to have all of the other pieces in place before you can see the whole picture.

Forgiveness has scientifically proven health benefits; not only does it helps promote both the quality and quantity of life, and generally improves a personal sense of well-being. Hanging onto anger, hatred, guilt, and remorse is toxic and tends to destroy and eat away the person that is unable to let go of the experiences that created this emotional poison in their system. Negativity likes to hang out with like-minded souls, so where you find one negative emotion, you can guarantee the rest will be close by, waiting to join in. If the person who created this inability to heal yourself is no longer in your life what greater satisfaction could they get than to know they still retained the ability to destroy your life you have taken on the role of your own abuser, willing to destroy your health and well-being in the process.

Those who say they can't forgive either don't know how to because they lack the necessary knowledge and understanding to do so, or don't want to forgive, because they feel their anger and hatred is justified and forgiveness is letting them off from the consequences of their actions. If the person who generated such toxic emotions in you is such a bad person, they won't give a shit about your feelings, and take a perverse satisfaction from the fact that the only person being hurt by such heart based negative emotions is you. How would I feel as a victim of a violent attack on myself or a loved one? The honest answer is I don't know, and neither does anyone until they are faced with that reality. High ideals and principles are wonderful things to discuss as moral concepts, but life has the habit of stripping them away and presenting us with real life situations and demanding an answer to the question ''now, what do you really stand for'' Neither can I predict how another person will react based on my beliefs and values, nor can I use ''human nature'' as an excuse for my need for revenge.

An eye for an eye leaves us blind to the truth that violence spawns further violence, with each atrocity worse than the last, justified by the minds of men consumed by the need for greed,

244

power, and control, clever enough to ensure that others pay the ultimate price.

Violence never brings peace, it simply postpones the moment when the killing must stop and the peace process begins, enemies sitting side by side, with dialogue replacing the bombs and the bullets. The healing process asks us to forgive not forget or condone, not so much as letting the past go, more leaving it where it belongs, a memory of what was, not a prophecy of what will, or must be. On a personal level as adults we can never be a victim without our consent or participation, it's our ignorance and fear that empowers others to treat us in a way we believe we deserve. Its only when we begin to change our perception of ourselves can we break free from the negative victim mentality. Once we begin to change we are faced with the task of forgiveness, forgiving ourselves for the mistakes we made before we knew any better, and forgiving others whose actions were the catalysts for our change and personal development. Part of that personal development asks us to step back and cultivate the ability to look at the much bigger picture and to put recent events into context.

We as individuals may not be responsible for recent events in the world, but our foreign policy and government actions are a major contributing factor. If we choose to sell weapons to countries that openly support, finance and arm the terrorists, we shouldn't be surprised when they turn those weapons against us. If we choose to declare war on sovereign states for political and financial gain killing tens of thousands of innocent civilians in the process, is it any wonder that people blame us for the actions of our government, actions carried out in our name, and feel they have just cause to retaliate. There is no justification in their action or our own, yet both are justified in their own eyes by the nature of the hidden agenda that motivates their actions. Wars are never fought for truth and justice; they are motivated by greed, power, and control and once set in motion they develop an energy all of their own expressed by revenge, retaliation, and retribution. All of which is good for business.

While war is profitable, peace and those who advocate it won't be invited to sit at the table with the power brokers. There is a time for forgiveness, but first must come knowledge and understanding so we can recognise the lessons to be learnt, change in such a way that forgiveness becomes possible and appropriate allowing peace to become a reality and the healing process to begin.

Chapter 41 - If you have the right, you also have the responsibility

Some people are very quick to shout about the violation of their rights when they feel they are being treated unfairly, but rarely if ever do you hear those same people claim ownership of their responsibilities. It's as if we have become a society where the rights of the individual are no longer set by legal, social or humanitarian standards, instead the term appears to have been customised to justify the individuals claim to whatever they want regardless of whether they have earned it, worked for it or are entitled to it. Their mantra is ''life and society owes me, and refusal is a violation of my rights''.

Rights don't appear by magic; every right you can lay claim to has been bought and paid for by others, often at a price that required them to forfeit their own life and rights so you can enjoy the benefits you now claim ownership to. Life and society owes us nothing; and it's naive to expect life to be fair, to act responsibly and treat everyone the same when we refuse to live by those standards ourselves. Life doesn't just happen as if by magic; it's created, we create it, and what appears to be unfair or unjust is usually the result of actions taken by those who believe they have the right to do so, without thought or consideration of the outcome of their actions. Fairness is impossible without the capacity to act responsibly, unfortunately responsibility can't be given, it must be accepted in the hearts and minds of those who understand the true cost of any right is the responsibility in which the right is earned and exercised.

Change cannot be divorced from life for it's the very fabric of life itself. Change is evolutionary or revolutionary and only we can choose. Comfort is warm, and certainty is secure; it's the sedative that robs us of the will and desire to change. Change has sharp edges and an uncomfortable fit; that can appear dangerous and uncertain. Change is nothing more than life in motion and those who would hold us to the belief in selfishness and personal mediocrity make liars of us all, those who believe them make liars of themselves.

Chapter 42 - We must choose what defines us

We must choose what defines us; if not, we will be at the mercy of the tides of emotion and circumstance, pulled in the direction of whichever one exerts the greatest control. The power to choose not only gives us direction; it also gives us authority to create the life we want to experience. Our thoughts, beliefs and values are the motivation of our actions, and it's through our actions we are judged by others. Change the thought and you will ultimately change the belief and values that then arise from that new mindset, this change in the thought process allows us to change direction of our personal journey. Apathy allows us to drift, unconcerned and indifferent to what is going on around us.

Safe in our personal bubble, our sphere of perception that creates our fragile reality, we exercise our right to stay silent and distance ourselves from the collective responsibility of the global problems we face. Our silence is deafening in the face of wide scale corruption and injustice, and we seek to ease our conscience in good deeds and worthwhile causes that make us feel good about ourselves without ever going beyond the limits of our comfort zone. *"I work for a living and I pay my taxes. I recycle all of my trash and attend church on a Sunday religiously, what more can I do"?* As long as you believe this is enough there is nothing more you can or will want to do. What we focus on, what it means to us and what we choose to do about it defines who we are. These three things are instrumental in the development and strength of our personality and character, they help us find our voice and the courage to speak out for those unable to speak for themselves. Those who choose to stay silent in the face of injustice and oppression for the sake of their own peaceful life are condoning the actions of others in the mistaken belief that it's not their responsibility and there is nothing they can do to change things.

What we focus on, what it means to us and what we choose to do about it defines **who we are.**

Change can be challenging, uncomfortable, and frightening but change is life in motion, a necessary process that empowers our personal development as individuals and our evolution as a species. Without change, development is impossible and we would be still living in a dark age where oppression is accepted as a legitimate means of control, and where power and greed are deemed the property of the elite. Politicians and religious leaders make peace redundant sacrificed to the profits of war, and the belief that one God is more powerful than another demanding the sacrifice of the faithful followers' but never those who instigate the call to war. Global problems will never be resolved until we accept a personal responsibility for the state of the world we have collectively created, or allowed to be created in our name. The burden of crippling guilt is not a pre-requisite but a comfort zone that no longer fits is a good indicator of a mind awakening to the realities of life. Sometimes being made to feel uncomfortable is a necessary price to pay to bring about the birth of a new idea.

Chapter 43 - A good Yin is nothing without its Yang

Those of us that think about such things would say that given a choice we would prefer to be considered a good person rather than a bad one, and have all of the personal qualities needed to make us so. We readily accept all of the good things about ourselves and reject anything within us that may be viewed as bad, negative or downright nasty. We don't like to think we could be any of those things and we are confident we are in some way different from those who are. It is easier to think of ourselves as fine upstanding people with all of the qualities that make us feel content in our own goodness and virtue. If the truth was told and we were honest with ourselves, we would have to accept that we all hold within us the ability to create both the light and dark side of our personality. This duality negates the "either or" and replaces it with the "I am".

Holism asks us to look at the whole person whether it is for health or personal development, when we do this; we can make the mistake of looking at the perceived whole good person and rejecting the darker side of our human nature. Understandably we would much prefer to concentrate on our good points and hope that the not so good stuff takes the hint and goes away of its own accord. Unfortunately, the more we deny the shadows of our character the more determined they are to gain recognition. If we try to suppress parts of our own nature we automatically create resistance to our own actions. Suppression creates both pressure and resistance and parts of our nature, the shadows we deny will struggle for recognition and acknowledgement. If we are not careful this can lead to a release that is both uncontrolled and damaging.

By recognising the **shadow** in its own right, we direct the light of our awareness towards it and its resistance is dissipated and neutralised.

We all have the capacity for both good and evil. All virtues contain within themselves the seeds of all vices and taken to the extreme any virtue becomes unstable and problematic. Balance requires us to accept all parts of our nature, the good and the bad and recognise that potential of any kind requires action on our part before it can be fulfilled. We have control over which part we wish to feed, develop and grow. If we wish to develop the good side of our character, we do so independently of our baser qualities and not at their expense. By recognising our negative qualities we negate their power of control over us through their internal struggle for acceptance and recognition. Failure to accept the holistic view of our nature can lead to a major conflict within us that can be dangerous and destructive. In some cases, the more talented and gifted the individual the greater their capacity for self-destruction. The brighter the light that shines the darker the shadow it casts.

Lofty virtues cast even greater shadows and the more you focus the light of your awareness on those virtues the more intense the shadow becomes. By recognising the shadow in its own right, we direct the light of our awareness towards it and its resistance is dissipated and neutralised. This process restores balance between capacity and potential, what we are and what we can become. We all contain within us the ability and potential to be saint or sinner, and from our limited knowledge and understanding we strive to be one or the other, without realising that it's only in acknowledging this duality can one gain meaning, perspective, balance, and control.

Chapter 44 - To a closed mind, an open door is a barrier it can't pass through

Freeing the mind can be very liberating, as we reclaim our personal power through the letting go of other people's beliefs and values, and more importantly stop taking responsibility for other people's actions. It's also personally empowering to ask the question; is what I now believe about myself supporting my idea of who I am, and who I want to be? This new mindset is liberating to budding free thinkers who want to understand and know their true self, but frightening to those who resist all forms of change and are addicted to the sedation of their comfort zone.

Conformity is a prison with many cells that seek to control, separate, segregate and divide, using the belief that we are defined not by our humanity, but by colour, creed, race and religion. What we believe determines our reality; our beliefs create structure and a platform from which we sit in judgement of those we consider different. Lines drawn in the sand soon become entrenched and then defended against an enemy of our own making, while the real enemy of humanity goes unnoticed. Conformity becomes our prison; ignorance and fear are our jailors, but knowledge and understanding provides the key to our release. Before we try to fit in with others we must first learn to honour our own space and when you do you can never be lonely if you like the person you find within that space.

Chapter 45 - Religion, reality shows and celebrity status

Religion the great enslaver of minds once held the monopoly on all things spiritual, but as science gained a foothold it began to challenge the churches version of events and offer a different take on the universe and story of the creation. In many ways religion has failed to address the important issues of modern day living and the stock in trade response of *"its God's will"* is no longer acceptable in a technological age where ignorance like faith, is a matter of personal choice. Once something becomes a commodity it becomes open to exploitation as are the people who literally buy into a product that is on offer at a very reasonable and justifiable price.

The higher the price the greater the perceived spiritual value on offer and those who can afford exorbitant amounts are encouraged to feel elevated and privy to esoteric knowledge not available to those in a lower income bracket. The medicinal salesmen of old are alive and well, they still offer a cure all at a price, but now they are image conscious and understand the finer details of public relations. Their image and the success they offer is as much a part of the product as is the information they present as the key to everyone's future success. Take something simple and make it appear unduly complicated, then charge for the pleasure of making it appear simple again. If you have the advantage of celebrity status it becomes a guaranteed success as people become blinded to the truth by the brightness of the glitz and glamour before them.

Knowledge and understanding are power and the more we understand about ourselves and the universe we are a part of the more informed and educated we become. Spiritual knowledge and understanding are not the same as academic or vocational expertise. Mainstream education is not set up to free minds, it's an institution designed to condition developing minds to think in a way that maintains the status quo and sustain society's structure and power base. When a society is governed and controlled in a way that demands obedience, conformity and the acceptance of the idea that the right to govern comes as a birthright of the privileged, a mind that can think for itself becomes a clear and present danger, and more of a threat than a violent revolution.

What we are spoon fed as news and stories of interest by the media is controlled by the conglomerates who own the media. The banks big businesses exert pressure and control over politics and the politicians in order to maintain and strengthen their power and control. They have a vested interest in creating what we see, hear and subsequently believe to be true. This willingness on our part to accept a life that has taken on a 'reality show' persona means without thinking, many are ready and willing to accept a spiritual placebo that lacks real substance but has the effect of softening the edges of life and keeping us trapped in a mundane existence. TV and the reality it creates has become the opium of the masses.

When we think of value it invariably equates to material possession and it can be argued that you can't put a price on knowledge and understanding. This is true to a certain extent and a problem arises when the spiritual concept tries to make the transition into the written word. Mainstream publishers don't own the monopoly on spirituality, quality or content; their remit is one of profitability and the number of copies they can sell so there is always a trade off between commercialism and a sound spiritual message that lacks a high profile name or falls outside of the publisher's field of interest or expertise. When achieving a place on the bookshelf or the best sellers list becomes the over ridding priority the content although well written may owe more to marketing than the spiritual content of the book, or the life experience of the author.

Thinking alone won't set anyone free. The ability to think simply allows us to revisit what we already know and accept to be true. If we want to change we have to take personal responsibility for our own development and sooner or later begin to question and challenge what we believe in, and hold to be true. While the questions of who, what, why, and when may be universal, the answers discovered within ourselves may set us on totally different paths to this spiritual awareness. This is how it should be; no single path stands higher than another or is any way more spiritual than it's contemporary. If our destination is enlightenment through the acquisition and application of knowledge and understanding of self, then our priority must be to allow our faltering steps to take us where they lead safe in the knowledge that the universe and the life it provides are the ultimate teachers of the student who is ready and willing to learn.

One of the greatest spiritual teachers comes free of charge and is available all year round whenever its help and guidance is required.
Mother Nature has the power to heal and educate on so many levels!

One of the greatest spiritual teachers comes free of charge and is available all year round whenever its help and guidance is required. Mother Nature has the power to heal and educate on so many levels; walking on deserted windswept seashore has the power to clear the mind and provide perspective like nothing else can do. Time spent walking in the countryside eases both mind and body as the stresses and strains of a hectic lifestyle simply melt away. A flowing stream or river encapsulates the flow of life, and with the ability to sit quietly allowing our senses to tune into the life giving energy around us, a clarity of mind and spirit is the gift we are given. A forest provides the opportunity to sit at the feet of a great and powerful teacher; to sit in silence at the base of a mighty tree is to experience the earth's life force as it effortlessly creates and sustains the life that we enjoy and take so easily for granted.

If spirituality is a meaningful activity that brings about change, growth and a re-formation of the personality then getting to know ourselves, this stranger that lives our life becomes the most spiritual and liberating thing that we can do. Knowledge and understanding are power and the more we come to know and understand ourselves the greater the control we are able to demonstrate in the creation of a life free from the limitations imposed by religious or media generated conditioning, ignorance and fear. The how we do it isn't as important as having the courage and determination to venture into the unknown, trusting that the universe is both willing and able to guide out faltering steps.

Chapter 46 - Sorry you are .... who?

When the next atrocity happens as it will, Facebook will again be awash with flags and the obligatory ''we are and we stand with'' statements and pledges of support and unity. Before we rush to join in should we not first take a moment to stop and think about what we are about to do and most importantly ask ourselves why. Are we doing it because it's a good and righteous thing to do? Are we doing it because we are caring and compassionate, socially and morally aware of life going on in the world? I ask not to offend but to question the thinking behind our actions no matter how well intentioned they may first appear. Once you have posted a flag and made a statement of unity you have made a choice, but more importantly you have also made a judgement call against those you chose not to support or stand behind in their hour of need. Where do you draw your line, who is worthy of your compassion or deserving of your hatred and mistrust? Are your choices based on personal values of what's right and comforting for you, or is it ignorance and fear, if they are then we must first ask ''who are we, and what do we stand for''?

The media seeks to form and direct public opinion. Its agenda is very simple, to strengthen and maintain its power and control over what we see, hear, read, and believe, but in real life the bad guys don't always wear black. Righteousness isn't restricted to those who we believe to be good, death and destruction leaves no one with clean hands or a clear conscience, the good and the just stand on both sides in any conflict. How we view this particular truth depends on which side of the line we choose to stand and whose banner we stand behind. Is one life worth more than another because of the colour of its skin or its status or place of birth? Is gay pride any more righteous than straight pride or any other "pride banner" you care to follow. The media would have us believe that Islam is a threat and we dutifully point the collective finger of blame until events challenge our perception of image and stereotype we hold to be true. Celebrity status no matter how fickle has the power to change values in an instant. The late and great Mohamed Ali was a Muslim and a great athlete, and there was an outpouring of grief and sadness at the loss of the 'greatest'. He was a Muslim a follower of Islam but in our eyes he was seen as a 'good guy', so that makes it different doesn't it?

There is nothing wrong with posting a flag and saying "we are" but is the flag kept aloft by the strength of public opinion or by personal values based on sound knowledge and understanding.

Chapter 47 - The critical mass of enlightenment

The term critical mass is borrowed from nuclear physics where it refers to the amount of a substance needed to start a chain reaction. Once the chain reaction is established it becomes self perpetuating growing in proportion to the energy contained within its expansion. In social terms, this same critical mass is achieved when a sufficient number of people are willing to accept a new and innovative ways of thinking so that the rate of social change becomes self-sustaining and creates further growth of new ideas and values.

In personal terms, critical mass is achieved when we have invested sufficient time and energy into our own development and we begin to experience a change in our sphere of perception. Our commitment to change becomes less laboured as we begin to experience incremental improvements which create a momentum of their own. With this freeing up of movement comes an easing of rigid thought processes, and a willingness to think outside of the box we have allowed ourselves to be confined to. Each step forward no matter how small takes us inexorably closer to the point in time when we reach our own critical mass of personal transformation. This personal transformation is part of a much bigger picture as it plays its part in the evolution of the human consciousness on a global scale. We are all part of the collective consciousness and as such personal development is never conducted in isolation, no matter how alone you may feel.

On a planet that is home to approximately eight billion people we are quickly reaching the point where a complete social, political, religious and environmental makeover is desperately needed. Regardless of your personal beliefs in the origins of mankind and the length of time we have inhabited this planet the fact that we have lasted so long without totally self-destructing is either nothing short of a miracle, or the old ways with all of their inherent faults, got something right. Unfortunately, if we use the past as a template for the future we are guaranteed to repeat our past mistakes instead of learning from them, and while the old order may provide us with a degree of comfort and nostalgia it's no longer stable enough to build a future upon. It's been estimated by some teachers and new age thinkers, that the critical mass of the global population is less than one percent which when reached, will trigger a chain reaction of growing personal and collective awareness. Once established, like any chain reaction it will become self-perpetuating growing in proportion to the mass of new knowledge and understanding that becomes available. While the figures required to reach this point of critical mass can be argued and debated, what is beyond question or doubt is that the old ways no longer work and we are quickly running out of time to come up with a viable solution to these problems.

A new order, a new way of thinking, a new set of life affirming beliefs and values are necessary to ensure our continued existence on this planet and each and every one of us must play our part in bringing this about.

A new order, a new way of thinking, a new set of life affirming beliefs and values are necessary to ensure our continued existence on this planet and each and every one of us must play our part in bringing this about. We no longer have the luxury of sitting back and waiting for someone else to do if for us. The clock is ticking. We can wait for the inevitable conclusion to the way life is headed, or we can contribute in our own way no matter how small, in the investment of our future and of generations to come.

History if it still exists will judge us accordingly. Our evolution as a species has brought us to a crossroad and we must choose individually and collectively if we wish to stay on a path that will lead to an inevitable conclusion, or choose a route less travelled that requires us to break new ground and old beliefs in equal measure. Those who ask 'but what can I do' fail to understand the power of their contribution, no matter how small or insignificant it may appear. The challenge before mankind is monumental but a journey no matter how great is never accomplished in giant leaps and bounds, rather it's the repetition of small often wavering footsteps, which delivers us to our final destination. Each one of us has the power to make a difference in life whether we realise it or not but to do so we must first change the way in which we think. Thoughts are the parents to our beliefs and actions, change the nature and quality of our thoughts and we begin to create a new reality that has no option than to manifest in our lives. We are part of a collective consciousness and as such we are never as isolated as we may think, and when we find the courage within ourselves to step up and accept a personal responsibility to make a difference and move us inexorably closer to that critical point, we empower others to do the same and the balance is redressed.

No one can know for sure if the figure of less than one percent of the total population of the planet will be the tipping point that allows the critical mass to be realised. What is certain and beyond any doubt it exists, it awaits our arrival and a single positive thought, a life affirming belief or an action motivated by love and compassion instead of ignorance and fear must one day deliver us to that pivotal place of enlightenment, knowledge and understanding. A single step moves us ever forward; a single grain of sand can tip the scales in our favour and a single thought, belief or action has the power to transform life beyond all recognition and who is to say that you can't be the one to do it.

Chapter 48 - Now is the time to reclaim your personal power

Anyone who has ever been used, abused or victimised will know what it's like to feel powerless. That cold and desolate place of fear and self-loathing we learn to live with and come to accept as our own. When this is 'learned' as opposed to institutionalised and imposed, it becomes second nature and takes on a life of its own. An abused child will more often than not grow up to feel powerless as an adult, even if those who took power from them are no longer alive, or a part of their lives. This early negative conditioning forms a mental and emotional blueprint that we look to replicate in other aspects of our lives. In doing so we may replace one abusive role model for another.

The abusive parent is replaced by the domineering partner, husband or wife who finds themselves promoted to a position of power and authority. Without realising it we can sometimes become our own worst enemy and we must take great care that when the abuser has done with us, we don't continue where they have left off. We can do this by keeping oneself locked into forms of self-abuse or harmful compulsive behaviour. Our thoughts become toxic and through them our psychology becomes our biology and the powerlessness is internalised. To reclaim that personal power, we must first understand the processes involved so they become meaningful and more than a loose fitting casual concept. We need to understand what the different elements look like before we can search for them. In every situation there is something for us to know before there is something to do, it's this increase in knowledge and understanding that is the first step in any healing process. The first tentative steps in reclaiming our personal power begin with the healing of oneself. Healing yourself is the ultimate demonstration of personal power and control.

Healing is education by another name and if we want to reclaim our personal power then we must educate ourselves first and foremost. All users and abusers know instinctively or intellectually that knowledge is power and the key to freedom and it's in their best interest to keep us locked into the darkness created by ignorance and fear. Knowledge and understanding brings the light of clarity by which we are able to see that much of their perceived power is illusionary made real by our belief in their dominance, fear and our lack of personal power.

We all have legitimate entitlements that are formulated by our human rights. We all have the right to live a life free from physical, mental, emotional, and sexual abuse. And while these can be considered our birthright they still need to be understood, valued and at times defended against those who would deny us the freedom they bring. We have the right to be treated with respect and to express ourselves freely. Most importantly, we have the right to ask for what we need and to defend that right should it be unfairly withheld or maliciously denied. Our voice and our ability to speak up for ourselves is an outward expression of our personal power. Unfortunately, when we are robbed of our personal power we can lose our ability to speak out against the injustice that we face. Finding an alternative means of expression through the development of a new skill and ability can lead to the rediscovery of our voice and with it the courage and ability to speak our own truth. Success can have a very liberating effect and help us find the confidence to stand on our own feet and seek rightful recognition for who and what we are.

The sting of another's inconsideration is painful enough, but when the abuse is deliberate and sustained the pain and resulting trauma can last a lifetime. Sometimes the damage is so great that professional help is required before any form of personal development can be even be considered and put into place. If we need it then we must ensure that we get it. No matter what form it takes professional help must initiate the empowering process whereby we feel able to take the first tentative steps in reclaiming ownership for our life one right at a time. If we slavishly believe that others have the power to set us free we will remain trapped in a prison of our own making.

Relying on faith, hope or the charity of others as our saviour is misplaced and does us the greatest dis-service. It works on the premise that others alone have the power to free us from feeling powerless thus creating a self-defeating vicious circle. Actively seeking advice and guidance is not the same as passively sitting back and waiting for someone else to tell us how to live our lives. We must ultimately take responsibility for our healing, education and personal development.

Reclaiming personal power requires a change to take place and begins with a healing of the self. This is only possible when knowledge and understanding is present for healing of any description is impossible without it. To achieve this, we need to change our focus. Instead of looking to others for praise, permission, or validation we need to look inward, because that's where we will find the answers we are looking for. Healing of the self begins the moment knowledge and understanding becomes a greater influence than the ignorance and fear that appears to be in control of our life. When we begin to heal ourselves we have begun our journey towards the reclamation of our personal power. Yes, our thoughts can be toxic but by the same token they can also be the most up lifting and life fulfilling resource at our disposal. This reclamation is an incremental transition because knowledge and understanding never comes to us complete. Each step leads to the next, success builds upon success thus providing us with a solid foundation.

> Instead of looking to others for praise, permission, or validation
> we need to look inward, because that's where we will find the answers we are looking for.

Personal power is made up of many components, self-respect, self-worth, trust, courage, strength, love, and compassion and these elements are reflective of the individual's needs and personal circumstances they may face. Each has to be worked at to be secured before it can be put into place. Often the most difficult element to reclaim is the power of forgiveness. Primarily the forgiveness of self for being a victim and for any guilt or misplaced responsibility we may feel. We must also reclaim the power and ability to forgive others. To forgive is not about condoning what they did or freeing them from responsibility. We forgive so that we are released from their control over us, and the consequences of their actions.

Although the feeling of powerless creates a void in our life it never leaves us completely empty. It leaves a residue of negativity for what we give up or have taken away from us is replaced with anger, guilt, frustration, anxiety, and self-loathing. All of which we must come to recognise, accept and release before we can begin to heal. With the lack of power come hopelessness and despair and the belief that the situation is permanent and beyond repair. Those who use the abuse of power to victimise help cultivate these feelings of isolation to satisfy their own needs, feed into their own sense of inadequacy and maintain their control over us. To reclaim our personal power, we must first become aware of the fact that we have either given it away to others or it has been taken away from us by those with the strength, position or authority to do so. Then we must be willing to accept that it can be reclaimed and we are capable of making changes in our thoughts, beliefs and actions to create the necessary transition.

A major part of this personal reclamation is the act of letting go. This apparent contradiction is a powerful step in the process. The letting go of debilitating beliefs creates the space in our hearts and minds for personal power to find a home, become established and grow into a new powerful life fulfilling reality.

Chapter 49 - A global solution begins with personal responsibility

Whether we like it or not we must all accept personal responsibility for the state of the world we are now living in. A global responsibility that equates to a social awareness and ultimately a personal responsibility to bring about the changes necessary to guarantee a world fit for future generations. Packing our bags and moving away from the problem isn't an option, and if the time ever came when a space age Ark 2 became a possibility, current human nature being what it is, it's fair to say places would be allocated not with the intent of saving the species, but based on position, power and status. Premier VIP class would be the order of the day, and everyone else written off as expendable and left to fend for themselves among the ruins of civilisation. If you feel this kind of decision would never be allowed to happen simply open your eyes and you will see these kind judgement calls being made every single day on a global scale. Life has become a very cheap commodity unless you have power, wealth, and prosperity to protect you from the realities of life in the 21st century.

We are a human race living in a large global village that is shrinking by the day. Where once upon a time travelling large distances would take weeks and months, the same journey is now completed in a matter of hours, and information takes longer to type than it does to travel around the globe. The more technically advanced we become the more ignorant and unconcerned we appear to be about the consequences of our actions, and the affect they have on the planet that sustains us. Politicians, world leaders and financial power brokers are making short term decisions in order to generate further wealth and prosperity for themselves, decisions that will have lasting and long term negative effects on generations to come.

War, corruption, and the pollution it creates in the hearts and minds of those it touches is big business. When war generates trillions of dollars worldwide peace has no value in the eyes of those who see no further than the profit to be made from the next conflict. When pollution is seen as an acceptable price for progress and the destruction of wildlife, trees, rivers and oceans, is written off as nothing more than collateral damage, conservation is simply viewed as an irritation that is paid lip service for the sake of public relations, and then totally ignored, and it's business as usual. Division is a means to an end. Generated and manipulated, created in order to divide, influence, and control. Politics, religion, and wealth are the great dividers that segregate and alienate. Once we buy into this belief it becomes easy to convince us that we have something to fear from those who we are conditioned to believe are different from us.

Colour, creed, race, and religion are just some of the many categories and stereotypes used to reinforce the belief that we have nothing in common with the people we share our home with. This planet is our only home and the people we share it with are not neighbours to be ignored because we think they are not our kind of people, they are a family we must learn to get along with if we want to secure a life and tenure for future generations. Each one of us has the power to make a difference and that difference begins in our own minds and the way we think.

Education is the key to change and the mind that can think for itself and has the courage to break free from its own ignorance and fear is the greatest threat to those who would seek to control the world's resources, the environment, society and the world as we know it. The individual is only powerless as long as they believe themselves to be, each one of us can bring about change in our own lives which must then impact on the lives of those around us. In a universe composed of energy a small solitary action on our part has the power to create a ripple that has a lasting effect and far reaching consequences. In standing up for what we believe to be right; in speaking out for those who are unable to speak for themselves, in helping those less fortunate we make a difference. Every time we refuse to accept bigotry, hatred, and abuse we give strength to others and help them make a stand against insidious forms of injustice. There may be times when we are a lone voice and find ourselves standing alone against what appears to be overwhelming odds but it's at those times we come to realise what's important to us and what we are prepared to stand up and be counted for.

The planet we live on is the only one we have and whether we like it or not each and every one of us has a duty of care to do our best to look after it. A responsibility to leave it in a fit state for those who have to come after us, a responsibility that we can't negate for it's our life and we alone can live it. We are not asked to become environmentalist overnight, or political activists ready to overturn corrupt governments, we simply need to become more aware of the world we live in and make changes in our own lives that reflect this new level of consciousness. We are energy beings whose fabric is that of the universe, any changes we make no matter how small must affect both the global and universal consciousness for in reality, there is only one conscious mind on this planet that we call home.

The planet we live on is the only one we have and whether we like it or not, each and every one of us has a duty of care to do our best to look after it.

Chapter 50 - When the blood red poppy is no more

As I stood at the grave of an Unknown Soldier I bowed my head in respect and silently gave thanks for the sacrifice he and so many of his fallen comrades had made. My moment of quiet contemplation was brought to an end as a soft and gentle voice broke the silence. *"Such a waste of life"* Lost in my own thoughts, I failed to hear a veteran approach and stand next to me. I turned to face him as I said I wanted to take a moment to pay my respects and leave a Poppy as a token of my gratitude for what they did.

"Ah the poppy of remembrance; less you forget us. We gave so much and you give us a blood red poppy in return as a token of your appreciation"

I'm sorry I don't understand!

"That is why you have to make more and more poppies every year. You still don't understand or have learnt the lessons from history that demanded our sacrifice. Your gratitude is a wonderful thing but there is little point in remembering us if you fail to learn from our deaths. In life war is the ultimate obscenity and no amount of poppies will ever change that. We did not give our lives to be honoured by an artificial flower, but to help you recognise the futility of war so that you would never have to pay the price that we did. In that we have failed you. If you wish to

honour the fallen bow your head, say thank you for a time when you will choose peace over war, and the blood red poppy is no more''.

Then he was gone and I was left alone with my thoughts. I looked around at all of the headstones and wondered if the day will ever dawn when the lesson is finally learnt and Remembrance Day becomes a day of celebration of peace, when war and the blood red poppy are no more.

Chapter 51 - Conclusion

There you go; you made it to the end. A short but hopefully informative journey during which, if I have achieved what I set out to do, you will have gained a broader and much deeper appreciation and understanding of what ''Reiki'' is, and how it can be taught in a contemporary way that is relevant to the needs of the 21st century.

I hope you noticed there wasn't a ''Love and Light, Namaste or Peace and Blessings'' in sight, there were however, a few references to shit, bollocks and bullshit. ''Spiritual'' buzz words are often used to imply a greater level of understanding than actually exists; unfortunately the use of spiritual catch phrases doesn't automatically create spiritual people. On closer inspection we often see a veneer that is wafer thin, and a reality that rarely if ever, lives up to the image, an image that requires high maintenance to stop the cracks forming and revealing the true nature hidden behind the mask.

There is nothing wrong with using these words as long as you understand their true meaning, and more importantly why you feel the need to use them. They only become meaningless when our actions don't reflect the true spiritual meaning of the words, or in the mistaken belief that their use elevates us in the eyes of others. Actions will always speak louder than words, and the greatest sermon is that which is lived, not preached to others.

Actions will always speak louder than words, and the greatest sermon is that which is **lived**, not preached to others.

There are those who believe Reiki is primarily for good and deserving people of the world, those that can afford it, and deserve it by nature of them not being "bad" people. Their desire to make a difference is determined by which charity appeal has the highest profile and fits in with their social sensibilities. Their love and compassion takes many forms; measured and well thought out to ensure they stay within a comfort zone that is never challenged or threatened. Their forgiveness comes at a price, but is negotiable. They bask in the glow of their own good deeds, and avoid the darkness at all costs. Little do they realise that ignorance and fear come in many guises; the greatest teachers are found not in the spotlight of the celebrity or the warmth and comfort of adulation, but the darkness where many "good and spiritual" people fear to tread.

It's in these places we find those who are hurt and damaged, who challenge our beliefs and preconceived ideas about who is worthy of our love and compassion, our help and forgiveness. It's easy to love those who make us feel safe and secure, who love us in return, but our metal is tested when we are faced with those who are broken in mind, body and spirit, who experienced ''love'' in the form of violence, abuse and neglect. Damaged children who became damaged adults still trapped by the fear, and angered by their own vulnerability and robbed of their personal power. Adults unable to set boundaries and say no to selfish and unreasonable demands made by those who should love and care for them.

I have cried with them and shared their nightmares; I have watched them stare into the distance knowing they are reliving a memory they alone can see. I have listened to their stories and found the words within my own pain to lift them from the depths of despair, and bring them back from the brink of the abyss that threatened to overwhelm and swallow them whole. These are life's survivors; worn down by hardship, bruised battered and scarred. Burdened by misplaced and undeserved guilt, bowed but never broken, deserving of much more than spiritual platitudes, no matter how well meaning they may be. These are my kind people, for when I hear their stories and answer their request for help, it re-enforces my belief that this is what Reiki really looks like, stripped back and totally devoid of all pretence and empty promises of miracle cures.

Do I have faith in its ability to help transform lives? No, because faith is a poor substitute for knowledge and understanding. I know from my own experience and that of my students the energy we work with, no matter what label we chose to place on it works. It's neither intrusive nor dictatorial; its unconditional and responsive to our needs and if we can just find the courage to step up and do our part, it will always take care of the rest.

My thanks and gratitude,

Phillip

Appendices

Training Qualifications and Education

Edexcel Advanced Diploma in Health and Social Care Level 3

Edexcel Intermediate Diploma in Health and Social Care Level 3

CFA Business Administration Level 3

CFA Certificate in Business Administration Level 2

City and Guilds Information and Guidance Level 3

NCFE Certificate Safeguarding Children and Young People Level 2

NCFE Certificate in Mental Health Awareness Level 2

Level 2 in Numeracy and Literacy

ICS Apprenticeship in Customer Service

PCET Diploma in Education

NCFE Certificate in Managing Diversity Level 3

NCFE Certificate in Equality and Diversity

PCET Certificate in Education

Certificate in Counselling Skills

Reiki Master Teacher Trainer

Trainer Assessor: D 32 & D 33

Diploma in Management Studies

Certificate in Management Studies

Certificate in Supervisory Management

Short Training Courses

MAPA Training Instructor Certificate

Safe Talk Suicide Awareness

Working with Personality Disorders

MVA Training

Autism Spectrum Conditions

Nutrition

Mental Health: Deprivation of Liberties

Production and Implementation of Support Plans

Medication Operating Procedures

Dave Hingsburger Lecture

Handling and Issuing Medication

Health and Safety in the Workplace

Manual Handling

Emergency First Aid at Work

BAFE Fire Training Certificate

E-learning Courses:

Personality Disorders

Safeguarding Adults and Children

Responding to Emergencies

Health and Safety

Information Governance Awareness

Infection Control

Equality and Diversity

Active Care

Dealing with Concerns at Work

Safeguarding Vulnerable Young People

Child Protection Awareness in Education

IFL-NSPCC Child Neglect Level 2

IFL-NSPCC Safer Recruitment Level 2

IFL-NSPCC Preventing Bullying Behaviour Level 2

IFL-NSPCC Children's Rights Level 2

IFL-NSPCC Child Protection-Staying Aware Level 2

IFL-Child Sexual Abuse Level 2

IFL-First Aid Essentials Level 2

IFL-Protecting Vulnerable Adults Level 2

IFL-Health and Safety in Education Level 2

IFL-Personal Safety Level 2

IFL-Samaritans Work Life Stress Management Level 2

IFL-NSPCC Child Protection Awareness in Education Level 2

Epilepsy Awareness

Medication Administration for Care

Mental Capacity and Deprivation of Liberties Safeguarding

Safeguarding of Vulnerable Adults Level 1

Dementia

Equality and Diversity Level 2

Foundation Health and Safety-Care

Knowledge Set for Medication

Knowledge Set for SoVA

Knowledge Set for Dementia

About Phillip Hawkins

Phillip Hawkins is a practicing psychic medium. He has been practicing Reiki since 1999, and he's been a Reiki teacher since 2000. In addition to teaching, when time allows he gives talks and leads discussion groups on the above topics. Applying Reiki on a daily basis has transformed his life and continues to do so as each day brings with it a new and deeper understanding of Reiki and of life. Phillip would like the opportunity to share that knowledge experience with others in an open minded and non judgemental way in a Reiki Rays 'community of enquiry'.

Made in the USA
Columbia, SC
24 January 2018